MAR 2 1 2017

ON THE LOOM

A MODERN
WEAVER'S GUIDE

BY *Maryanne Moodie*

PHOTOGRAPHS BY *Alexandra Grablewski*

ABRAMS | NEW YORK

CONTENTS

INTRODUCTION

I HAVE ALWAYS LOVED vintage textiles. The youngest of six, I spent a lot of time with my siblings in charity shops, scouring the racks for secondhand clothes and toys. The experience was like being in Aladdin's cave—you never knew what treasures lay beneath the next layer. Even as a child, I was drawn to handmade, heavily embroidered, and sequined fabrics and clothes, all of which caught my eye and fired up my imagination. As I grew, I loved them more because I began to notice and appreciate the marks that the past had left on them—some darning here, a replaced button there—clues that they had been loved, a little hint that there had been lives lived alongside these beautiful treasures.

I began my career in teaching, much of it in art education, and I taught for more than ten years. I loved teaching art, because it allowed me to impart both knowledge and skills, as well as share in the joy of creating with my students. The most exciting aspect for me was observing how every student brought his or her own unique vision to each task, and I enjoyed seeing how differently everyone interpreted and applied the skills I shared. But I still couldn't get enough of textiles, so alongside my teaching career, I began to build a small business sourcing and selling exquisite vintage clothing and homewares. Both paths taught me so much about building a community, being open to opportunities, trusting your instincts, forgiving yourself, and the logistics of running an honest and environmentally sustainable business.

Then I became pregnant with my first son, Murray. When the time came to go on maternity leave, I needed to clean out the art storeroom. This took me back to my days of childhood charity shopping—there was treasure to be found under the years of layers. Beneath the piles of paper and supplies, I discovered a small loom that was intended for the trash bin. Although I didn't really know what it was or how it worked, something spoke to me on a deep level: The loom connected with my passion for vintage and my desire to create. There was a hole in

the top of the box, so I wasn't even sure if the loom had all of its parts, but the conviction was strong, so I rescued it.

Being at home as a new mother can be one of the hardest and most isolating times, and it can be challenging to your energy, sanity, health, and sense of self. After my son was born, I found myself struggling to adapt to a new life with a different identity. I was no longer a teacher. I had put my business on hold. And I was exhausted and overwhelmed.

One day in 2012, as my little babe slept, I remembered the loom. I pulled it out and read the instructions. I didn't have any yarn, so I warped up the loom with jute and used waxed neon cord to weave myself a swatch of fabric. Immediately, I was hooked. That small instruction manual didn't get me far, so I started teaching myself new techniques from snippets I found on the Internet, and finally I moved on to vintage weaving textbooks sourced from eBay and used bookstores. My beginning as a weaver was a fumbling comedy of trial and error. I would bumble along and "invent" new stitches, only to discover later that generations of weavers had been using that same technique for hundreds of years. I pored over vintage textile inspiration and tried my hand at creating different effects. Every time I sat down to begin a new piece, I would push myself to try a new skill, incorporate a new fiber, and mix colors in unexpected ways. I wanted to draw deeply on the nostalgic quality of vintage wall hangings while breathing fresh life into them with surprising color and texture combinations.

Weaving turned something on inside me. I felt like I wanted to know more, do more, be more involved. So I began sharing my work on social media, to try to connect with other artisans. Immediately, I received supportive feedback from a community of amazing women. At first, most of them were customers from my vintage-clothing business, who already appreciated the aesthetic of a woven wall hanging with vintage roots. But slowly, my tribe grew. Through the Internet, I began making connections with other weavers, spinners, dyers, and makers. I discovered a whole community of people out there who had been able to make meaningful connections, support one another, and grow together. I felt like I was coming out of the darkness and being welcomed into my new identity as a mother and a maker. It felt great.

As time went on, I was able to draw on my experience teaching in the arts, my passion for weaving, and the joy of community-making by sharing my knowledge in sold-out workshops around the world. I like to keep the vibe of the classes accessible to complete novices as well as people who want to get back into working with fibers after a long absence. Just like in my art classroom, I encourage people to find their own voice. I teach everyone the same building blocks or skills and watch, excitedly, as they use these skills to create new and unique projects that are all very different from one another. I encourage my students to "weave weird" and try to push the boundaries of what they think is possible. By sharing my knowledge, I am able to learn through my students.

Now, as much as I would love to, I could not possibly travel to all of the wonderful cities in the world to share my knowledge in person. Everyone needs to start somewhere when learning a new skill, and the best place is at the beginning. When I first started weaving, I had no one to talk to about how much I loved it, or to discuss where to find resources, or to celebrate tiny achievements. My husband says that I've built a weaving cult for the purely selfish reason of wanting to talk about weaving and fibers with like-minded people. He's right. So this book is for you—let it be your entry point or introduction to weaving, a book of inspiration that teaches you and helps you to begin and to find your own tribe. Get your looms out, flip to a place in this book that piques your creative interest, and get ready to make some new and exciting projects!

GETTING
STARTED

TOOLS
AND SUPPLIES

WEAVING TREADS THE LINE between art and craft. As a craft, there are enough rules to follow to get new weavers into a comfortable rhythm, while giving rule-breakers many opportunities to have a little fun. As an art, the umbrella of styles, fiber options, and project types is so wide that anyone can create a piece that suits their particular taste—minimalists can create clean projects in neutral tones, experimentalists can create explosions of color and texture. But regardless of why you want to get into this craft, first you have to learn the basics!

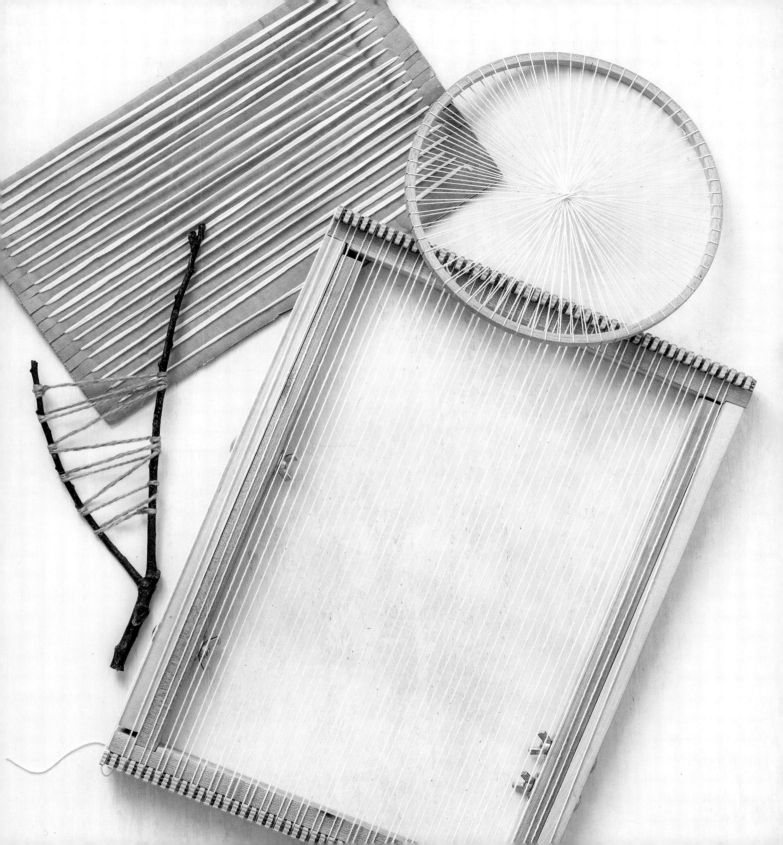

LOOMS

ALL WOVEN PROJECTS START WITH A LOOM. A loom an essential part of the weaving process—it is the structure that stretches and holds your framing threads (also known as the warp; see page 24) organized and held at the right tension, while you interlace or weave your other threads (weft) into them. This is how the final fabric, or cloth, is created. When you are done with your weaving, you typically remove your project from the loom and display it separately. Hence, a loom is a tool used in weaving and does not necessarily remain with the final product.

There are many different types of looms ranging from simple, like frame looms, to complex, like floor looms. Frame looms, which are handheld looms, are the most basic and most widely available. They're sturdy, portable, and inexpensive, making them a great first loom for a beginner weaver. In this book, we'll be focusing on projects that can be made with rectangular frame looms, circular frame looms, and even "looms" made from found objects like branches or cardboard.

PARTS OF THE LOOM

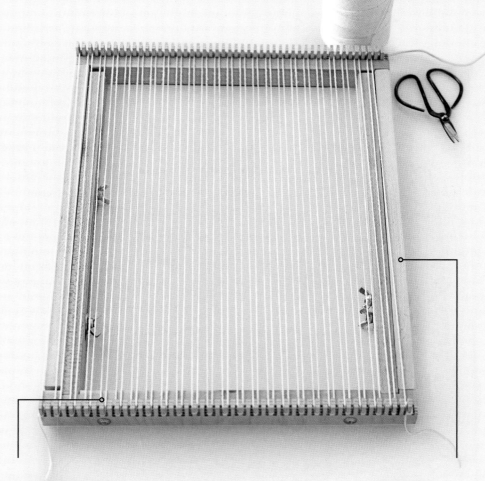

TEETH OR PEGS

The teeth, or pegs, are the notches along the edge of the frame that allow you to wrap the warp thread at even intervals, keeping it in place for your weaving. The number of teeth relative to the loom's width determines the density of the woven fabric.

FRAME

The frame of your loom is the rigid outer structure that holds the shape of the weaving you're creating. In a typical frame-style tapestry loom (for instance, in all of the projects featured in the Rectangular Looms chapter on page 42), your weaving will be only as large as your frame.

WEAVING TOOLS

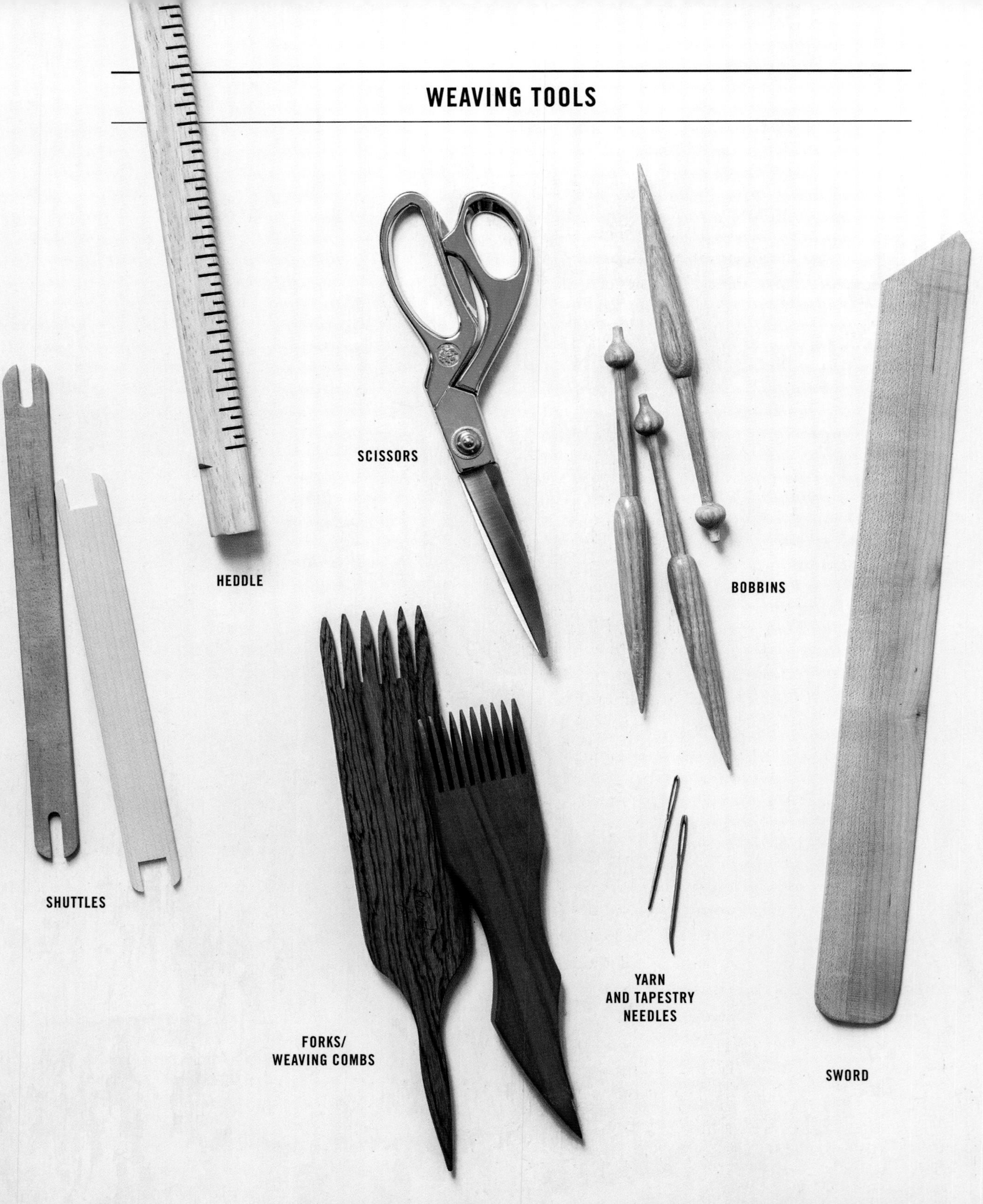

SHUTTLES

HEDDLE

SCISSORS

BOBBINS

FORKS/
WEAVING COMBS

YARN
AND TAPESTRY
NEEDLES

SWORD

01 YARN AND TAPESTRY NEEDLES

Tapestry needles are an important part of the weaving process. You use them to guide the weaving yarn (weft) over and under the warp threads, and that creates each row of your weaving. A tapestry needle differs from a standard sewing needle in a few important ways: it's much larger, has a blunter tip, and most important, it has a large eye that allows the thicker yarn to pass through. Many tapestry needles also have a bent tip, which helps you to pick up each warp string faster.

02 SHUTTLES

A shuttle is a tool that holds a long length of yarn while you weave, so you don't have to repeatedly rethread your tapestry needle, as you would if you were to use shorter lengths. To load a shuttle, you wrap yarn around the base lengthwise, laying it inside the notches at every pass until the shuttle is as full as you'd like. Then, you trim the yarn, leaving a long tail to weave with, and use the shuttle to guide the yarn tail through the warp. You can use this in combination with a weaving sword (see right) for extra-speedy weaving. (The shuttle is used in place of a needle, so you can cover a larger area at a time.)

03 BOBBINS

A bobbin is a tool for storing the yarn you're using as you weave. In weavings of many colors, separate bobbins are used for each color, so you can switch easily between different yarns. Bobbins are used in the same way as shuttles or needles. Shuttles are used to cover the largest areas, bobbins are used to cover smaller areas and for looping stitches, and needles are used to cover the smallest and tightest areas.

04 FORKS/WEAVING COMBS

A weaving comb, or fork, is used to evenly push down each row of weft fiber as it's completed. You can use your fingers to "beat down" the row, but a fork can help your piece look more tidy, even, and tightly woven.

05 SWORDS

A weaving sword, or shed stick, is another tool that helps speed up the weaving process if your project is comprised of mostly tabby stitch. To use the sword, weave it into your piece as if it were a piece of yarn, then turn it onto its narrow edge to open up a shed—the space between your upper and lower sets of warp strings. This large, open area allows you to quickly pass your weft yarn through the warp and to complete an entire row of tabby stitch in one movement. (Swords will open the shed in one direction only. You must still weave in the opposite direction.)

06 HEDDLES

Like a sword, a heddle is a tool that can be used to separate warps to open up a shed. The genius of the heddle lays in the alternating grooves that allow the weaver to open up sheds to weave in both directions.

MAKING A SHUTTLE

A shuttle can be a very helpful tool when weaving large areas of tabby stitch (see page 26). To make your own, cut a small rectangle out of a piece of cardboard. For a standard sized loom, I use a shuttle that is approximately ½" x 8" (1.3 x 20.3 cm). For larger projects where you will use a lot of bulky fibers, like the scarf on page 61 or a rug, you can cut your shuttle base a little larger, to approximately 4" x 10" (10.2 x 25.4 cm). Once you have your base, cut wide V-shaped notches in each short end. The notches will help you to wind more yarn without it getting bulky.

CHOOSING
YOUR FIBERS

YARN COMES IN MANY DIFFERENT textures, materials, and weights. When you are beginning a new project, it's good to think about how you want your end product to look. Will it be organic or modern? Colorful or monochrome? Different fibers offer various characteristics that dictate both how you weave and the result. Thinner yarns give you a very neat, defined look, but take much longer to weave. Thicker, handspun yarns offer a softer, more organic look and are quick to weave up, but you won't be able to create designs with sharp, defined shapes or lines. Natural fibers treated with natural dyes offer a soft and subtle color story, while manmade fibers colored with synthetic dyes create a more vibrant result. I always think it is best to experiment with as many different types of fibers as possible to find the ones that resonate the most purely with you and can best help bring your vision to life.

RAYON

COTTON

MOHAIR

SHEEP'S WOOL LOCKS

HANDSPUN SHEEP'S WOOL

JUTE

SILK

ALPACA

ANGORA

RAFFIA

COTTON DENIM STRIPS

SHEEP'S WOOL ROVING

LINEN

NATURAL vs. SYNTHETIC FIBERS

I USE A VARIETY OF FIBERS FOR MY WEAVINGS, but I tend to use natural fibers more often than machine-made fibers, because I find natural ones are more interesting. I like the inconsistencies in hand-spun and hand-dyed fibers—not only do they create interesting textures, but the small differences in each type tell a story.

As such, most of my weavings are made from vintage and hand-spun fibers. In particular, I like to collect vintage machine-knitting cones that were once used in textile factories. Those factories' old inventories are a treasure trove of unusual and hard-to-find fibers. To add an extra dimension, I like mixing many fibers together in one woven piece—I use a lot of wool, cotton, alpaca, and silk in my pieces. Although I prefer to work with the natural fibers listed opposite and on page 20, sometimes I add synthetic or non-traditional elements to my projects—like rope, pieces of leather (faux or otherwise), or raffia—to make the texture more interesting.

In this book, the projects are made of either thread, yarn, or fiber. Traditionally speaking, thread is made of cotton and yarn from wool, while fiber can be any material. You'll have fun trying out lots of different fibers—just make sure that you only use non-stretchy fibers for your warp.

Natural fibers may be made of cellulose or protein. Cellulose fibers, like cotton, are made from plants, while protein fibers such as wool come from animals. What follows is a selection of the fibers I use most often in my designs. You can see them pictured on page 17.

CELLULOSE FIBERS

01 COTTON

Cotton is an extremely durable, but also very soft, fiber. It's a great choice for warp threads, and cotton-based yarns provide good definition in weaving. You can even weave with strips of cotton fabric! See the Rag Rug on page 51 or the Denim Catchall Basket on page 105 for how to use strips of cotton fabric as your base. Color choices abound!

02 LINEN

Linen is beautiful to weave with but is inelastic. Yarn that is made of, or includes, linen often feels very silky and can appear somewhat shiny. Linen can make for a good warp, but beware—it doesn't like friction. Too much friction weakens the fiber and causes it to break. Linen is best used in smaller projects. If you want to use lengths of linen fibers in larger pieces, it is best to use them doubled.

03 HEMP

Hemp is one of the most durable cellulose fibers. It starts out very coarse but softens up as it's handled. Due to the porous nature of hemp, it retains color very well and can be dyed easily to match your project. You can use it for both weft and warp.

04 JUTE

Jute is a long, soft, and shiny fiber. It is also very durable and one of the most affordable fibers out there. When jute is woven, it creates a burlap-like material. You can use it for both warp and weft, which creates a very toothy fabric.

05 RAYON

I'm referring to rayon as a "natural" fiber because it's made from wood pulp, but it undergoes such extensive processing before it becomes a fiber that it's usually considered synthetic. Rayon feels like cotton and is great for colorwork, as it sucks up dye really well to create lovely, bold colors.

06 SHEEP'S WOOL

Sheep's wool is probably the most common fiber I use for weaving. This type of wool is elastic, resilient, warm, and takes dyes easily. My favorite sheep's wool is hand-spun, and I prefer to buy naturally dyed fibers from small-batch producers, to give a more unique, organic look to my pieces. I also like to work with unspun sheep's wool, like locks or roving, to add different textures to my design.

07 SILK

Silk is the strongest of the natural fibers. It is breathable, hypoallergenic, and luxuriously soft. I love weaving with recycled silk strips in place of yarn. It adds the kind of bulky texture that can only be achieved by weaving with a ribbon shape. With silk you have many color choices, as seen in the projects on pages 65 and 92.

08 ALPACA

Alpaca is a soft, durable, luxurious, and silky fiber. While similar to sheep's wool, alpaca is warmer, not prickly, and it has no lanolin, which makes it hypoallergenic.

09 ANGORA

The wool from Angora rabbits has a soft, thin fiber with a fuzzy halo, an effect that's even more obvious in woven fabric. While much warmer and lighter than sheep's wool, angora isn't naturally elastic, so it can be used for warp or weft. Angora is continuously renewed and gently harvested during the Angora rabbits' natural molting process; thus, the Angora rabbit need never be harmed for its wool. Thank you, rabbits!

10 MOHAIR

Mohair is the wool from Angora goats. Like Angora rabbit wool, it is a soft, thin fiber that feels luxurious while also maintaining integrity and durability. Mohair's fuzzy nature gives a stunning fluffy halo to your weaving projects.

FIBER WEIGHT

MOST BOOKS AND YARN MANUFACTURERS rely on standard terms to indicate a yarn's weight (thickness). Here are the most common yarn weights you'll encounter when shopping for your projects.

THIN .... THICK

LACE   SUPERFINE   FINE   LIGHT WORSTED   MEDIUM   BULKY   SUPER BULKY

LACE
The lightest weight of yarn

SUPERFINE/FINGERING/BABY WEIGHT
A very lightweight yarn used for socks, items for children, and delicate projects

FINE/SPORT WEIGHT
A lightweight yarn used for throws, items for children, and sweaters

LIGHT WORSTED/DK WEIGHT
Used for lightweight adult items

MEDIUM- OR WORSTED-WEIGHT/ AFGHAN/ARAN WEIGHT
One of the most popular yarn weights, great for all types of projects

BULKY
Heavier than worsted weight; builds up quickly

SUPER BULKY
Double the weight of worsted, or Aran, yarn

WEAVING
BASICS

YOU COULD STUDY WEAVING for many years and still not scratch the surface. I weave every day and learn new things every time I sit down at the loom. Although there are many different stitches and methods for creating woven projects, I have tried to give you the simplest, quickest methods for getting started. Here, I've outlined the stitches and skills that I use the most to create a little weaving basics sampler (you can try your hand at all of these stitches by making the Woven Wall Hanging Sampler on page 47). Use it as a sort of cheat sheet. Once you've mastered these techniques, you can continue to learn new stitches, tips, and tricks from vintage books and online tutorials, or by joining a weaving guild in your area.

WARP AND WEFT

ALL WOVEN PROJECTS ARE MADE UP of the same two elements: the warp and the weft. The warp threads serve as the underlying structure of your weaving—they run up and down, wrapped around the pegs of the loom, and thus create a base of vertical lines to weave into. Weft threads are then woven through the warp threads widthwise (horizontally) to create cloth.

PARTS OF THE WEAVING

WARP THREADS

Warp threads establish the basic structure or shape of your weaving. Wrapped around the loom's pegs, warp threads form the base of vertical threads that you can weave weft fibers into. Your warp threads should be made of strong, non-stretchy yarns that don't break easily. The best way to determine a good warp yarn is by applying a "snap test." Give your warp yarn a sharp tug—if it breaks or pulls apart easily, you'll want to try a different material. Good examples of warp threads are mercerized cotton (also called cotton rug warp), linen, rayon, and jute.

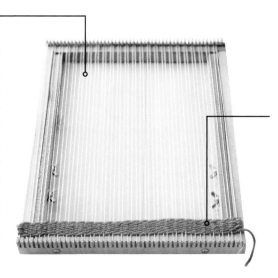

WEFT THREADS

Fibers that cross the warp in alternating over-and-under rows are known as the weft threads. Any fiber—stretchy or not—can be used for your weft threads. Choose fibers based on the effect you want to produce in your piece. See pages 19–20 for examples of what I like to use in my weaving projects.

BASICS
WARPING THE LOOM

01   The first step in weaving is to set up your loom! Holding a rectangular tapestry loom so that the pegs are at the top and the bottom, tie the end of your warp thread around the loom's bottom left peg. (A)

02   Draw the warp up and around the top left peg, then down again to the next peg in the bottom left corner. (B)

03   Continue the process until you reach the bottom right peg, then tie the warp in a double knot to secure it. (C + D)

04   Snip any excess warp, leaving a short tail.

BASIC STITCHES & DECORATIVE ELEMENTS

Once your loom is warped, you're ready to weave! Here are a few of my most-used stitches and techniques for creating one-of-a-kind pieces.

TABBY STITCH

Tabby is the most basic weaving stitch, and is the easiest to create.

01 To start, warp your loom. Thread your tapestry needle with a piece of yarn that is two arm's lengths long. Begin the stitch at the bottom right, weaving under the first warp thread and over the second, from right to left. (A+B)

02 Continue "sewing" the yarn over and under the warp threads until you reach the end of the

row. Pull the yarn through, until there is about a thumb's legth of yarn trailing from the place where you started. (C)

03   For your second row, start weaving from left to right above the row you just created, but this time, weave over then under, so that this row wraps the warp threads opposite to the first row. (D)

04   Be careful as you pull the yarn in this row—you want to be sure that it nearly touches the edges of your outer warp threads but doesn't pull on them or hang loosely. (A good way to make sure your tension is right is by using the "bubbling" method I describe on page 33.)

05   Continue on in this manner, switching the orientation of your weft with each row. After every few rows, beat down the stitches with your fingers or use a weaving fork to create a really tight weave.

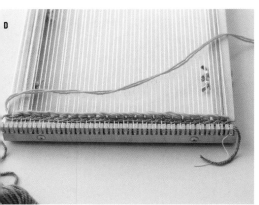

SOUMAK STITCH

Soumak is a diagonal looping stitch. When worked in two-row increments, it creates a row of stitches that look similar to knit stitches.

01   To start your soumak, cut a piece of yarn that is two arm's lengths long. Fold the yarn in half and loop it around the first two warp threads on the right. (A)

02   Then, tuck the end of the yarn behind the next two warp threads. Lightly tug your loop toward the base of your weaving. (B+C)

03   Continue on, passing your yarn under pairs of warp threads until the end of the row, tucking your yarn underneath the last two warp threads. (D)

04   To create a second row of soumak above your last row, skip the first two warp threads and lift the third and fourth warp threads from the left with your right hand, passing the yarn underneath from right to left. You will start to notice a V-shaped pattern in your weaving. (E)

05   As you finish the second row, do soumak on the last stitch, then pull the threads to the back of the warp. (F)

06   Weave in three rows of tabby above this row to lock in the stitch.

LOOPED TABBY STITCH

This looped variation of the tabby stitch is a great way to give your pieces textural interest. It looks best when created with a thick, chunky yarn.

01 First, weave a row of tabby; then, every time the weft crosses over the warp, give it a little pinch, pulling the yarn up and twisting slightly with your fingers. **(A+B)**

02 This will create little loops above your weaving, for a 3-D effect. **(C)**

03 Weave another three rows of tabby above it to lock in the stitch. From here, you can create a second row of looped tabby if you choose. **(D)**

RYA KNOT

Rya knots are stitches made from short, separate pieces of yarn that create a shaggy texture in your weaving. I like to begin my woven wall hangings with a row of rya knots to form a foundation for the piece, but you can also incorporate them randomly to add texture and interest to your projects.

01 To make a rya knot, cut four 6" (15.2 cm) pieces of yarn. Gather the yarn pieces together and fold the grouping in half.

02 Lay the U part upside-down on top of two warp threads, with the tails toward you. **(A)**

03 Bring the left tails around and under the left warp thread, and the right tails around and under the right warp thread. Pull both sides up through the space between the warp threads. **(B)**

04 Lightly tug the tails down (toward you), to set the rya knot. After completing a row of rya, always do three rows of tabby stitch above it to lock the rya knots in place. **(C + D)**

A
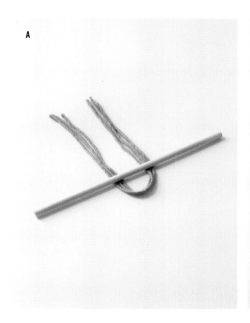

B

C

LARK'S HEAD KNOT

The lark's head knot is one of the most frequently used decorative knots in macramé, but I use it a lot in my weaving projects, too. It is used to attach or mount one cord or fiber to another, or to a ring or dowel.

01   To make a lark's head knot, fold one length of fiber in half (or use several lengths, as in the photos) and pass the loop underneath the place you want to mount it. (A)

02   Bring the looped section over the top of the base and pass both tail ends through the loop. Pull firmly. When tightened, the lark's head knot has a horizontal segment (made by the fold), which rests just below the mount point. (B+C)

TASSELS

Tassels are a quick and effective way to add a decorative touch to your work.

01 To make a tassel, wrap yarn at least twenty times around a piece of cardboard that is the length that you want your tassel to be. **(A)**

02 Cut a 12" (30.5 cm) piece of the same yarn and use it to wrap the wound fibers at one end of the cardboard. Tie the wrap off with a snug double knot and trim it to leave a 4" (10.2 cm) tail—this is the tie you will use to attach the tassel to your project. **(B)**

03 Cut through all of the bottom loops and remove the tassel from the cardboard base. **(C)**

04 Snugly wrap 30" (76.2 cm) of yarn near the top (tied end) of the tassel six to ten times. Tie the ends off with a double knot, then cut the yarn. **(D)**

05 Use a needle or crochet hook to hide the cut ends inside the tassel. Trim the tassel ends evenly and attach it to your work.

BASICS
TECHNIQUES

BUBBLING

A good way to make sure you are not pulling too tightly at the end of each row of tabby stitch (see page 26) is by using a method I like to call "bubbling." Bubbling encourages the weft yarn to wrap over and under each warp thread uniformly, so that your weaving has the proper tension.

01 Once you have completed a row of tabby, push your yarn up in the center to create an arc. (A+B)

02 Next, push the yarn down with your fingers in sections: first, scrunch down the center, and then push down each side, and finally beat down the whole row. (C+D)

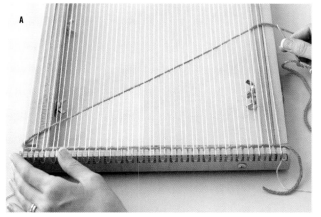

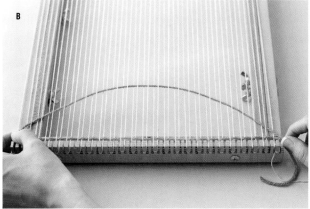

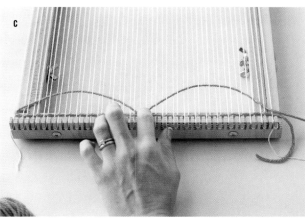

CHANGING COLORS
OR ADDING YARN

This is an easy technique to use when you run out of weft yarn and need to add more, or decide you want to change up the colors of your piece.

01 Lay your new piece of yarn behind the warp thread where you ended, cross it over the old piece, and carry on weaving in the same direction, making sure to bubble each piece separately. (A)

02 Leave a 3" (7.6 cm) tail for each yarn—you'll weave these in at the end (see opposite). (B)

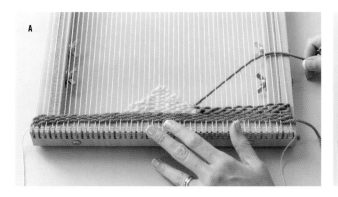

MAKING SHAPES

There are several ways to create shapes in weaving, but my favorite is a method known as diagonal slits, where you create slanted shapes with tabby stitches.

01 Weave a slanted shape, such as a triangle, in tabby stitch. Using that shape as a base, start to tabby stitch around it row by row. (A)

02 As you reach the edge of your base shape in each row, stop weaving when you reach the warp thread directly next to the shape (do not interlock the yarn or share a warp thread with your original shape). (B) When you reach the top of your base shape, stop, rethread your needle, and begin weaving from the other side.

FINISHING YOUR WEAVING

SURGEON'S KNOT

When tying a fiber off on itself, as in beginning or ending your warp, the method I use most often is my version of a surgeon's knot, or double knot.

To create one, take the tail or working end of your fiber and cross it back over itself. Pass it under the original fiber, and pull it up through the loop you created. Repeat, then pull firmly to secure it as you position the knot where you need it.

REMOVING YOUR PIECE

There are many ways of finishing a piece and taking it off the loom—the results vary depending on the project and the type of loom you are us-ing. But generally, all you have to do is pop the warp loops off the end pegs. If you are not hanging your piece, you can simply push a few rows of weaving toward the loops at either end to cover the empty space (the loops will keep the weaving in place and stop all your hard work from falling apart). If you are going to hang your piece, you will first insert a dowel into the top set of loops, and then gently push the adjacent rows of weaving toward the dowel to hold it in place.

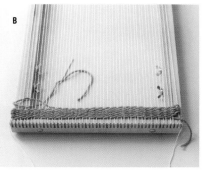

WEAVING IN TAILS AND ENDS

When you finish a piece, you'll be left with many little ends and tails, from when you started and finished, added new fiber, or changed colors.

01   To weave them in, thread your needle and work the yarn back into your piece for about five warps below the last row of stitches you created. Pull the yarn to the back of the loom. (A+B)

02   To neaten your work, you'll need to turn it over to the back and trim each tail to 3" (7.6 cm) long. Then, using a tapestry needle, a small crochet hook, or even just your fingers, work the tail back into the weaving vertically, over and under the wefts directly above or below it, but in the opposite direction that it had been worked. (C)

03   Work back through at least four to six warps, and then trim any excess.

COLOR DESIGN
AND HARMONY

COLOR CHOICE IS A VERY PERSONAL THING. What evokes a positive response in one person can just as easily make someone else feel ill at ease. We draw on our personal background, culture, and experiences when deciding if we like the way something looks.

While it's important to know the ways that different colors and shapes interact and how traditional color schemes are created, for most design projects you'll likely create custom palettes that don't strictly adhere to any predefined patterns. Be confident when choosing the colors for your projects—allow yourself to make decisions based on gut instinct and emotional response. If a specific palette moves you to "feel" something, then it will most likely evoke an emotional response in your audience. Here I'll teach you the basic rules so you can break them to suit your individual preference.

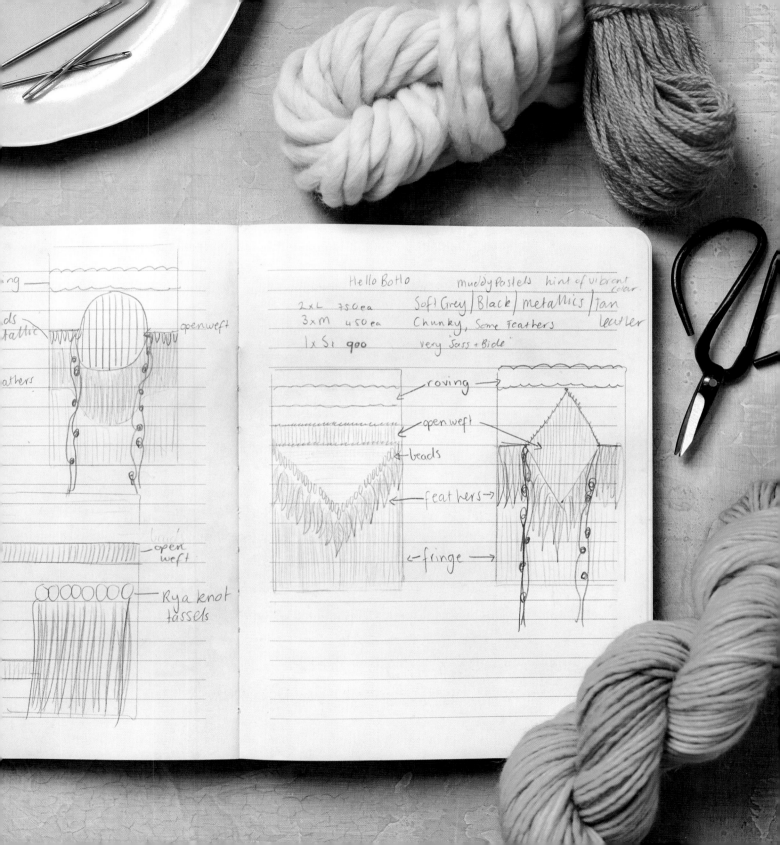

ng

ds
tallic

athers

open weft

open
weft

Rya knot
tassels

Hello Boho   muddy Pastels hint of vibrant colour.

2 x L   750 ea   Soft Grey | Black | Metallics | Tan

3 x M   450 ea   Chunky, Some Feathers   Leather

1 x S: 900   Very 'Sass + Bide'

→ roving →

→ open weft ←

← beads

← feathers →

← fringe →

WHEN YOU'RE CHOOSING YARN COLORS for your project, it's helpful to know the basics of color theory as it pertains to the color wheel. A color wheel is based on the primary colors: red, blue, and yellow. These colors are called "primary" because you can't create them by mixing any other colors. All other colors in the wheel are derived from some combination of these hues. Secondary colors are green, orange, and purple, and they are formed by mixing any two of the primary colors. Tertiary colors—blue-green, green-yellow, yellow-orange, orange-red, red-purple, blue-purple—are formed by combining a primary with a secondary color.

The following color combinations can help you hit the sweet spot every time. Try playing around with them to find your own pleasing palettes for your pieces.

01 ANALOGOUS COLOR SCHEMES

Analogous color schemes use three colors that sit side by side on a color wheel like a primary and the pair of tertiary colors on either side of it, such as blue-purple, purple, and red-purple, or a primary, secondary, and tertiary.

02 COMPLEMENTARY COLORS

Complementary colors are pairs of colors that are opposite each other on a color wheel, like red and green or blue and orange. You can expand your color scheme beyond the complementary pair by using tones (colors muted with gray), tints (colors lightened with white; pastels), and shades (colors darkened with black). Using complementary colors can be unexpected and jarring to the viewer.

03 NEUTRAL COLORS

I use neutral colors as the basis of most of my designs. Neutrals are frequently accented with brighter colors, but they can be used just as often on their own to create very sophisticated designs. When you choose a palette of neutral tones, it gives you a chance to play with elements of texture that become the focus of a design. Gray, black, white, brown, tan, and off-white are generally considered neutral colors.

04 MONOCHROMATIC COLOR SCHEMES

Monochromatic color schemes are made up of various tints and shades of the same color. These simple, classic color schemes are easy to create, as they're all closely related to the same primary or secondary hue.

05 — VIBRANT AND MUTED COLOR SCHEMES

Combining colors that have similarly muted or vibrant color schemes creates a sense of visual harmony. A piece using all vibrant or all muted colors can evoke a harmonious feeling. Adding a bright accent to an otherwise muted palette can be visually striking.

06 — WARM HUES

Warm hues include red, orange, yellow, and variations of those three colors. They suggest fire, fall leaves, sunsets and sunrises, and generally are interpreted as energizing, passionate, and positive.

07 — COOL HUES

Cool hues include green, blue, and purple and are often perceived as being more subdued than warm colors. They are the colors of night, water, and nature, and they are usually interpreted as calming, relaxing, and somewhat reserved.

Once you start playing around with colors, you will notice some quirks. A colored shape can look completely different against various backgrounds. Some colors appear more brilliant next to black than white. Others may look larger next to an analogous color but smaller and more brilliant close to a complementary color. The best way to figure out what you like is to just play around with your materials!

COLOR INSPIRATION

Although using the color wheel is a good start, I often get my best inspiration for color combinations from everyday life. Nature, in particular, is endlessly inspiring to me. Sometimes, nature comes up with unexpected color combinations that you don't necessarily find in traditional color theory, but for some reason they just work. When I'm feeling particularly stuck and need an extra dose of inspiration, I like to go for a hike, take a walk around the garden, or simply look at photos of nature online.

There are many other places to find inspiration, too. I like to look at archival photos of traditional costumes and swatches of vintage textiles. Take a walk along the street, and you will find color inspiration in street fashion and shop windows. Design and fashion magazines can be wonderful sources of ideas for combining colors that will create new and interesting looks. If you see a particularly interesting color combination in your daily life, try to take a photo or re-create it in a notebook. Organize your inspiration collection for later reference, to make all those color schemes more practical and easier to use in the future.

FINDING BALANCE & HARMONY

When applied carefully and thoughtfully, color theory can help you to achieve harmony in your piece. Using too many colors can result in a piece that looks busy or messy, but too few can end up boring.

Balance in art refers to the sense of distribution of perceived visual weights that offset each other. We feel more comfortable and find art most pleasing when the parts of an artwork seem to be in balance. Imbalance gives us an unsettled feeling, and that is something that, for most artists, is not the desired effect. Some artists, however, deliberately disturb our sense of visual balance.

You can achieve balance in two ways: symmetry or asymmetry. Create symmetrical balance in your piece by using identical parts, and the same number of parts, on each side of a design. Test whether yours is symmetrical by drawing an imaginary line through the center of your piece—does one side appear to be a mirror image of the other? Using symmetry makes your piece feel formal and ordered. Explore how the elements of design—hue, tone, shape, size, texture, repetition—can be played off one another so as to convey liveliness, variety, and informal visual balance. For example, a large, light-toned and textured shape, line, or area might be balanced with several smaller, darker ones.

WORKING WITH TEXTURES

Before beginning your project, it's a good idea to think about how the fibers you've chosen will behave once they are applied to your work. Sometimes, I make up small samplers with the fibers I intend to use in a larger project, to see if a particular material will work in the design I've created. Bulky fibers can vary in consistency, so they might be the wrong ones to use if you want to create a geometric shape with a clearly defined border. Very fine embroidery thread is perfect for small, delicate designs, but it would take a long time to fill in a large area, and it might break if you are challenging it to hold the structure of a piece, so you might instead use fine thread for decorations or embellishments. (See pages 19 and 20 for a full list of the fibers I like to use, and their individual qualities).

The best way to figure out which textures you like best is to explore and play with different kinds of fibers. You will soon figure out which ones work with your aesthetic and which ones don't.

RECTANGULAR
LOOMS

PROJECTS
IN THIS CHAPTER

RECTANGULAR, OR FRAME, LOOMS are typically used for rectangular or square projects. As the name suggests, this type of loom is made up of two shorter ends and two longer ends. These looms can have the teeth or pegs either only at the shorter ends, or around all four sides to give you some versatility in making a portrait or landscape piece. The size and shape of your loom is integral to the size and shape of your finished product. Although a rectangular loom will (mostly) result in rectangular weavings, you can, however, use this type of loom to make smaller weavings in different shapes. When you're through, just cut the shape off the loom, and weave each warp back in vertically to hold the desired shape.

MAKING A FRAME LOOM

There are a few different, and very affordable, ways to make your own frame loom.

The cheapest way is to use a piece of cardboard or matboard, as in the Woven Necklace on page 71. First, cut the cardboard to the size of rectangle that you want your finished project to be plus an extra 1" (2.5 cm) on all sides. Then, use a ruler and a pencil to draw a parallel line ½" (1.3 cm) away from each of the cardboard's edges; the area inside these lines shows the size your finished work will be. Measure out and mark the width of your "pegs." (I typically space mine ¼"/6 mm apart.) Make sure that the marks at the top perfectly line up with the ones on the bottom! Once you have the pegs marked, use a pair of scissors to make ½" (1.3 cm) notches at the top and bottom of your frame loom.

To set up the warp threads, leave a 3" (7.6 cm) tail behind the cardboard as you bring the warp thread into the first notch and down the front of the cardboard to the corresponding bottom notch. Wrap the warp thread behind that first "peg," then back up the front of the cardboard and around the next peg, just as you would use the pegs on a store-bought loom!

You can also make a sturdier and longer-lasting loom very affordably out of wood. To make a wooden loom, head over to your local art store and ask to see the stretcher bars used for painting. Then, decide what size you want your loom to be and pick out the corresponding stretcher bars (you'll need two for the sides and two for the top/bottom of your loom). When you get home, fit the notched stretcher bars together. (If you'd like, use a staple gun to connect the corners more securely.) To create the pegs, use a pencil and ruler to measure even spaces on the top and bottom edge of your loom. Then, hammer a finishing nail at every mark. To use your DIY frame loom, wrap your warp string around the nails as you would the pegs on a store-bought loom—voilà!

RECTANGULAR LOOMS
WOVEN WALL HANGING SAMPLER

WHEN I FIRST STARTED WEAVING, there were no online tutorials, so I did a lot of stumbling about in the dark, trying to figure things out from vintage weaving books and magazines. It took me a good year and a half before I felt like I had mastered the basic stitches, and even now, I still feel like I'm learning new things every time I create a new piece.

This tutorial is based on the syllabus from my popular beginner's weaving class. Here, I'm serving you all the stitches I learned in those first months of my weaving life in one bite-sized morsel. Bon appétit!

MATERIALS

- 12" x 16" (30.5 x 40.6 cm) rectangular loom
- Cotton rug warp
- 3—4 skeins yarn in the colors of your choice (see Note)
- Scissors
- Needle
- 1 or 2 dowels or brass rods, for hanging

Note: You'll need enough extra yarn to make some interesting rya knots, too.

01 Warp the loom. First, anchor the end of the cotton rug warp by tying it to the bottom left peg of the loom, leaving a 3" (7.6 cm) tail. Wrap the warp thread around each of the pegs on your loom, starting at the bottom left of the loom and finishing at the bottom right. Check your tension every couple of rows—you want the warp threads to feel bouncy, but not too tight. The warps of the top pegs will create a row of loops that will make it easy to hang your finished piece.

02 Begin to weave. Cut two lengths of your main color of yarn (I used white) as long as the span of your arms. Thread the tapestry needle, and weave tabby stitch from left to right. (These first few bottom rows are just to anchor your piece; later, they will be hidden by rya knots, so don't fret about the color you choose here.) Be sure to bubble your weft (see page 33), to ensure good, consistent tension throughout.

03 When you finish your first row, weave the next row directly above it, starting from the right side. Be sure to bring the yarn in this row over and under the warps so that they alternate with the first row's

warp threads. Check that the end stitches touch the first and last warps without bagging or pulling in.

04 Check your work after every few rows for accuracy, and be sure to beat down the stitches with your fingers to create a really tight weave. Continue weaving until you run out of yarn.

05 Create a rya knot fringe at the bottom of your weaving above the tabby base you just created (see page 30). For each rya knot, cut four to seven lengths of yarn, 9" (22.9 cm) each; the thicker the fiber, the fewer lengths you'll need. Make one rya knot for every two warp threads. Attach the rya knots to the bottom of your piece—one knot around every pair of warp threads—then trim the ends of the knots to the desired length. I cut my bulky-weight yarn fringe along a sharp diagonal line.

06 Once you have completed the rya-knot fringe, lock it in by weaving three rows of tabby stitch above it.

07 Create a second row of rya knots with yarns of various weights and

colors. Repeat steps 5 and 6, but this time, trim these knots into varied lengths and angles, to create some visual interest. Lock in

this fringe row with another three rows of tabby stitch.

08 Introduce woven shapes, using different colors and weights of

yarn. There are several ways to create shapes in weaving—one of my favorites is the diagonal slit rectangle (see page 34), which I've used here. First, you'll create a split rectangle with looped tabby stitch, working from right to left (mine is a soft coral color). Weave the diagonal edge by decreasing or increasing your row lengths by a few warp threads each time.

09 Now you'll contrast the split rectangle by working from left to right with plain (not looped) tabby stitch. End the weft thread after you weave the last open warp thread—the one that's right next to the edge of the first split rectangle. Don't interlock the two different threads or share a warp thread with the first split rectangle.

10 Each of my split rectangles is based on six rows of tabby stitch, but yours could be more or less, depending on how big you want it to be and the thickness of your yarn. Repeat steps 8 and 9, using a different color of yarn for your second split rectangle.

11 Mark the midway point in your design with two rows of soumak stitch (see page 29). Lock in the

stitch by weaving three rows of tabby stitch above it.

12 Repeat steps 8 and 9. I chose to repeat the color of my first split rectangle for symmetry, then tried a couple of new shapes. Finally, fill in the leftover space with tabby stitch. When you're three rows from the top, create and attach three more rya knots in the center of the weaving (I used a shimmery gold pima cotton).

13 Once your weaving reaches the top of the loom, pop the top loops off the pegs. Don't worry—the warp loops will hold the weaving in place. Flip the piece over and weave in all your ends (see page 35).

14 To hang the piece, pass a dowel or rod (or branch, or spoon—experiment!) through the row of top loops, alternating the over-and-under pattern with your last row of tabby. (I chose to weave in two dowels on opposite warp threads, so that they would hold each another in place). To hang the rod, tie a piece of yarn or warp at each end.

15 Lift up your weaving, and admire your work!

DESIGN YOUR OWN

Here, I've offered instructions for making the exact wall hanging shown opposite, but after step 2, the design choices are really up to you! Here are some options for designing your own, one-of-a-kind piece using the basics that you learned on pages 26 to 35:

To add dimension: Add more rows of rya knots (remember to lock them in with at least three rows of tabby stitch when you're through) or create new shapes.

To add interest: Introduce a different weight of yarn or a new color.

To add texture: Try the soumak or looped tabby stitch.

RECTANGULAR LOOMS
RAG RUG

IT DOESN'T TAKE MUCH to make a house a home. My favorite way to make my house feel cozy and happy is to make the things I need by hand. Sure, it's convenient to buy something from a big department store or online, but when you make something yourself, you have the chance to turn materials that are lying around the house into something personal and cherished.

Rag rugs are the perfect project for using up a pile of selvages, old sheets, torn blankets, or even to reduce a fabric stash. These make wonderful gifts, and handmade items always have the possibility of becoming family heirlooms. I made my first rag rug about a year ago, and I'm happy to say, it's one of my favorite things I've ever made. Cushy and wonderful, it's the perfect landing spot when you step out of the bath.

This tutorial is for a bathmat, but you can change the size of the loom to create an area rug for any room in your home.

. . . .

MATERIALS

- 18" x 20" (46 x 51 cm) rectangular loom, or stretcher bars in the same measurements
- Wood glue, pencil, ruler, hammer, nails (optional, for creating stretcher bar loom)
- 3 queen-size cotton sheets, or any thin recycled fabric, for your weft
- Scissors
- Shuttle (optional)
- Weaving sword (optional)

. . . .

01 Make the loom. If you are unable to find a larger loom, you can create one of your own using stretcher bars and nails. To make your own loom, attach the two 20" (51 cm) stretcher bars to the two 18" (46 cm) bars using wood glue to secure them in place. Using a pencil, mark notches ½" (1.3 cm) apart across the short edges of the frame. Hammer the nails in at

these points. I like to alternate the placement of my nails so that every other nail is ½" (1.3 cm) higher than the one before. This makes it easier to warp and keeps the nails from being too tight together.

02 Prepare the fabric yarn. Lay out a sheet, right side up, on a flat workspace with the short ends at the top and bottom. Use your scissors to make small slits every 1" (2.5 cm) along the bottom edge. Beginning at one end, use both hands to rip down along one of the cuts to create a 1" (2.5 cm) strip of fabric. (A) Repeat with the remaining snips (you'll need lots!).

03 Attach the strips. Cut a 2" (5.1 cm) vertical slit close to the right end of one of your strips. Repeat with a second strip on its left end. (B) Layer the strips' cut ends together with the second strip on top. Feed the uncut right side of the top strip underneath your layer and pull it up through both holes. Pull through and tug so that you have a solid join. (C) Don't worry if you have a few "wings" peeking out—you'll be weaving over them. Repeat with the remaining strips to make one long strip of fabric yarn.

04 Roll your fabric yarn into a ball, and repeat the yarn-making process with the remaining two sheets.

05 Warp the loom. Tie one end of your fabric yarn onto the top left peg of your loom with an over-hand knot. Warp your loom by bringing the fabric yarn down to and around the first bottom left peg, then back up, and so on. (D) Check your tension every couple of rows—you want the warp to feel bouncy, but not be so tight that it begins to pull on the pegs or nails. Tie off in an overhand knot, leaving a 3" (7.6 cm) tail.

06 Begin to weave. Beginning at the bottom left, take your first strip and begin weaving tabby stitch from left to right using a shuttle or your fingers. Weave as closely to the nails as you can. The warp has left little loops that will hold your weaving in place so you won't need to tie knots at the end.

07 Make sure to bubble each row of tabby stitch (see page 33). Be sure not to pull so tight that your rug becomes misshapen. After each row, your strips of fabric should touch the end warps lightly, without bagging around

or pinching them. If you notice that your fabric is pulling or bagging, redo that row.

08 As you finish each row, use your fingers to push your rows tight up against one another to create a really packed-in look. The tighter you push the rows together, the more fabric you will be able to push into the rug, giving it more integrity and structure. When you need to add a new color or fabric strip, make sure to cross the tails of the old and new pieces over each other (see page 34).

09 Stop weaving when you are 2" (5.1 cm) from the top of the loom. If you have pushed the fabric up against each row tightly enough, you should end up with a nice, solid woven piece that can easily be removed by pulling the loops off the pegs.

10 Find the perfect place for your cozy new rug, take your shoes off, and enjoy the fruits of your hard work.

A Cut slits along the short end of the sheet, and use your hands to rip strips of fabric.

B Cut 2" (5.1 cm) slits close to the ends of two of your strips.

C Layer the cut ends together and feed the uncut end up through your slits to create a solid join.

D Warp the loom with your handmade fabric yarn.

MOROCCAN BOUCHEROUITE RUG

BOUCHEROUITE RUGS are having their moment in the sun. They've been popping up on blogs, in design magazines, and in the homes of stylists and the stylish. Traditionally, these rugs are created with leftover fibers whenever raw materials are hard to come by. The mishmash of recycled fabrics in my version ensures an eye-popping array of colors and wild patterns—a beautiful and resourceful way to recycle.

MATERIALS

- An assortment of T-shirt yarn in the colors of your choice (about four cones), or a selection of old T-shirts to recycle
- Scissors
- Basic Rag Rug, size is up to you, either handmade (see page 51) or purchased (see Note)
- Crochet hook, size E-4 (3.5 mm) or larger

Note: This project builds on a rag rug that you've either made or purchased, in the size of your choice. Depending on your design (see step 02), you may or may not see portions of this rug, so plan accordingly.

01 Prepare the yarn. Cut your T-shirt yarn into 2" (5.1 cm) long strips, and sort them into piles by colors. If you are cutting fabric from old T-shirts, make sure the strips are ¾" (1.9 cm) wide and 2" (5.1 cm) long.

02 Plan out your pattern or color scheme. To make my rug, I began by looking at some ideas on the Internet to see what I was drawn to, and then sketched my design. The rugs I saw included stripes, diamonds, triangles, and zigzags, so I included these elements in my design. You should also decide how much fringe you want on your rug. Do you want to cover the whole rag rug base like I did? Or would you prefer to have patches of designs with the original rug showing through?

03 Create your design. Starting in the first section, use the crochet hook to pull one end of a strip of the T-shirt fabric under a warp thread from the existing rug base. (A) Tug on the ends of the strip to make them even (if you've cut the T-shirt material to the length

A Pull a fabric strip under every third or fourth warp thread using the crochet hook.

B Tug on the ends of each strip to make them even.

I recommend, there will be 1" (2.5 cm) of it on each side of the warp). **(B)** Continue pulling your strips up through the third or fourth warp thread in each row.

04 Once you finish a section of your design, move on to a new shape or section. Keep checking back in on your design as you work on covering the rag rug base, to make sure you are creating the effect you desire.

05 When you feel that your design is done, cut all of the strips down with scissors to create an evenly shaggy texture.

RECTANGULAR LOOMS
EVERYDAY TOTE

WITH TWO LITTLE ONES AT HOME, I find that I'm often running out the door at a moment's notice, so I stay prepared by keeping a big bag by the door packed with provisions for adventures and emergencies. This colorful, soft tote has enough room for everything we need (and a lot that we don't). I'm always getting compliments on my version of this bag, and it gives me a real thrill to tell admirers that I made it myself!

MATERIALS

- Basic Rag Rug, 2' x 3' (60.9 x 91.4 cm), either handmade (see page 51) or purchased
- Straight dressmaking pins
- Scissors
- Cotton rug warp
- Tapestry needle
- 3 yards (2.74 m) cotton rope, ½" (1.3 cm) diameter, for the handle
- Pompoms, tassels, or other embellishments (optional)

01 Start by pinning your rug into a bag shape. First, fold the rug in half, so that the ends meet. Most rag rugs look the same from the front or the back, but if there is a side you would prefer to show, be sure to work with the wrong side facing out. Pin each bottom corner along a diagonal, about 3" (7.6 cm) in from the corner. (A)

02 Using your cotton rug warp and tapestry needle, whipstitch each bottom corner securely, through both the front and back along your pinned line. Continue the stitching up the sides, leaving the top edge open. Turn your bag right side out and lay it on a flat surface.

03 Make the handles. Pin one end of the cotton rope so that it starts 3" (7.6 cm) in from a side seam and 3" (7.6 cm) down from the opening. Arrange the rope so that it forms a handle above the open end and then lies on the bag 3" (7.6 cm) away from the opposite side seam. Bring the rope down the side, under the bag bottom, and back up the other side, pinning it securely and keeping it parallel to the other side seam. Fashion a second handle to match the first one, then go back under the bag and up the other side, so that the rope meets and passes the starting end. Arrange the ends so they sit snugly beside each other and trim them

A Pin each bottom corner along a diagonal.

B Pin the cotton rope around and under both sides of the bag to make handles.

C Stitch the handles in place every 2" (5 cm) with cotton rug warp.

so they overlap as much as you'd like them to. I then unraveled the ends of my rope so they would appear fringed, but you can leave yours as is if you prefer.

04 Thread the needle again with cotton rug warp, and use an over-stitch to bind the rope to the bag every 2" (5.1 cm). **(B+C)**

05 If you'd like to add some swag to your tote, you can create or buy a few small tassels (see page 32) or pompoms, and tie them around the handle to give your bag a little personality.

06 Now pop in your essentials (and a few non-essentials, too!) and head out on an adventure.

CHUNKY SCARF

I LOVE WINTER FASHION—my wardrobe is spilling over with boots, hats, gloves, scarves, and wraps. I get a little tingle of anticipation when the first few leaves fall, and I am always one of the early adopters of the season's finds, sweating in late September under my layers of hand-knit, hand-dyed, and hand-woven loveliness.

This tutorial for my favorite chunky winter scarf is super fun and easy to make. Once you finish the first one, I bet you will want to make one to match each and every outfit.

. . . .

MATERIALS

- 12" x 24" (30.5 x 60.9 cm) piece of cardboard or handmade frame loom (see page 45)
- An assortment of yarns in the colors of your choice (about seven skeins), including at least one that won't stretch or break for warping (see page 24 and Note)
- Ruler
- Pencil
- Scissors
- Tapestry needle
- Shuttle
- Crochet hook, size E (3.5 mm) or larger (optional)

Note: Your warp yarn will become the fringe at the bottom of your scarf ends, so choose accordingly.

. . . .

01 Cut twelve 62" (1.6 m) pieces of the warp yarn and set them aside. Place your loom vertically on a flat surface.

02 Warp the loom. Starting at the left-hand side, wrap a length of the yarn vertically around the loom, tying it off at the bottom with a bow, leaving 5" (12.7 cm) tails.

03 Tie another length 1" (2.5 cm) to the right of the first one. Continue across the cardboard loom until you have tied all the pieces onto the loom. (A)

04 Prep your weft yarn by wrapping it around a shuttle, so that you can hold a lot of yarn at one time (see page 15).

05 Using your first color of yarn, thread the tapestry needle, and

A Warp the loom with 12 evenly spaced lengths of yarn.

B Start to weave from the bottom left. Once you reach the top, flip the loom over and continue weaving on the other side.

weave tabby stitch from left to right, starting at the bottom left corner of your loom. Be sure to bubble each row of your weft (see page 33) to ensure that you will have good, consistent tension throughout. Check your work after every few rows for accuracy, and be sure to beat down the stitches with your fingers to create a really tight weave—this will ensure you fit in as many rows as you can, so your scarf is nice and warm. **(B)**

06 Continue weaving tabby stitch, changing colors as you like. When you need to add a new color or piece of yarn, make sure to cross the tails of the old and new pieces over each other (see page 34).

07 You can also insert rya knots (see page 30) randomly throughout, to add extra fun and texture to your scarf.

08   When you reach the top of the loom, flip it over and continue weaving on the other side.

09   Once you've finished weaving, slide the scarf off the loom and weave in the ends. Then untie the bows at the bottom of the loom and lay your scarf flat. You'll have a long scarf with fringe at both ends!

10   On each side of the scarf, tie the loose ends into bunches of three to create tassels. If you want to add more rya knots to the body and ends at this point, work them in with a crochet hook.

11   Top off a favorite winter outfit with your one-of-a-kind scarf, and head out for some hot chocolate.

RECTANGULAR LOOMS

FABRIC STRIP WALL HANGING

THERE ARE MANY VARIATIONS of woven wall hangings. Although the version on page 47 is what typically comes to mind, this is a much simpler, more pared down, and quicker-to-weave version made with strips of fabric. The fabric is the foundation of this project—add visual interest by dip-dyeing or tie-dyeing before cutting it into strips, or use varying widths of fabric to add a real textural element to your weaving. You can also buy recycled-rag yarn instead, making this project much quicker to whip up.

MATERIALS

- Recycled rag yarn or fabric strips (we used about one skein of recycled silk)
- 9" x 12" (22.9 x 30.5 cm) standard wooden loom
- Scissors
- Ruler
- Cotton rug warp
- Scotch tape
- Two wooden dowels or brass rods, each ½" x 9" (1.3 x 22.9 cm)

01 Prep your materials. Cut an assortment of fabric strips into 15" (38.1 cm) segments (slightly longer than the width of your loom).

02 Warp the loom. Anchor the cotton rug warp by tying it to the bottom left peg of the loom, leaving a 3" (7.6 cm) tail. Wrap your warp threads around each of the pegs on your loom, starting at the bottom left of the loom and finishing at the bottom right. Check your tension every couple of rows—you want the warp threads to feel bouncy, but not too tight.

03 Begin to weave. Use your fingers to guide the end of one of your strips over then under the first row of warp threads on your loom, working from left to right. Continue passing the strip over and under each warp thread, until you reach the opposite side of the loom. Tug the ends of the strip so that they hang evenly on both sides. Push the yarn down toward the base of the loom with your fingers.

04 Weave the next row directly above the first, making sure to go over and under the opposite warp threads. Continue building rows on top of each other, letting

the ends hang off the sides of the loom. Check your work after every few rows. Be sure to beat down the stitches so that you create a really tight weave.

05 Once your weaving reaches the top of the loom, pop the top loops off the pegs.

06 To hang the piece, pass a dowel or rod through the row of top loops. When the dowel is all the way through, wrap the cut end of the topmost weft strip around the dowel rod. Use your tapestry needle to weave the end vertically back into your weaving. Do the same with the bottom loops and the other dowel, to evenly weight the piece. To hang the rod, tie a piece of yarn or warp at each end of the top dowel.

07 To add interest to your piece, you can add fringe to the bottom, as I did here. To add fringe, cut several lengths of cotton rug warp, and attach each to your bottom dowel using lark's head knots (see page 31).

08 Step back and admire your work!

RECTANGULAR LOOMS
DATE NIGHT BAG

MOST OF MY DAYS are spent lugging things around—scooters, strollers, blankets, laptops, looms—you name it. So whenever I get the chance to dump it all and take only the necessities, I do! My phone, keys, cards, and lipstick all fit perfectly into this little bag, which I like to use for date nights with my husband, a day at a music festival, or drinks and dancing with the ladies.

....

MATERIALS

- 4" x 6" (10.2 x 15.2 cm) or postcard-sized piece of cardboard (see Note)
- Ruler
- Pencil
- Scissors
- An assortment of yarn in the colors of your choice (about three skeins), including at least one that won't stretch or break, for the warp (see page 24).
- Tapestry needle
- 1 yard (91.4 cm) of narrow ribbon, leather, or cording (capable of fitting through the eye of the tapestry needle), for the drawstring

Note: If you'd like to make a larger bag, increase the size of your cardboard to your desired measurements.

....

01 Make your loom. Lay your cardboard piece vertically, and draw a line ½" (1.3 cm) down from, and parallel to, one of the shorter sides. Mark notch lines ¼" (6 mm) apart along the top edge, then cut along the marks to the ½" (1.3 cm) line with your scissors. Cut each strip at a 45-degree angle, to create angled spikes—these will be the pegs at one end of your loom.

02 Cut a narrow notch at the bottom left corner of the card. This will be an anchor for your warp thread.

03 Warp the loom. Tuck 3" (7.6 cm) of the warp yarn into the bottom-left notch so that the tail is at the back side of the loom—you will weave it in at the end.

04 Draw the warp thread up to the top left spike, wrap it over the spike, and pull it back down to the bottom of the card, close to the notch. Pass the warp down to the bottom of the cardboard and

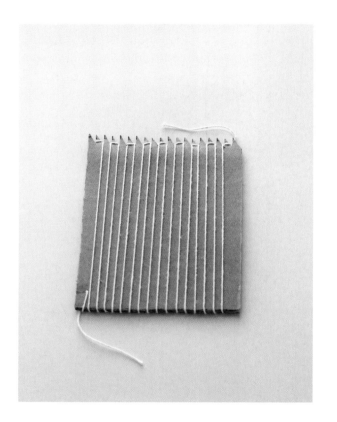

A Draw the warp thread up and around each notch on both sides of the cardboard loom and tie off.

B Weave tabby stitch in a spiral from left to right across the front and around the back of the loom.

back up to the other side (you are warping on both sides of the card). Wind the warp around the next spike to the right. Continue back down and around the bottom. At this point, check your tension—you want the warp to feel bouncy but not be so tight that it bends your loom. Continue until the entire piece of cardboard has been warped on the front and back. **(A)**

05 Tie the warp off at the top right spike and trim the tail to 3" (7.6 cm) long. This will be woven into your bag at the end.

06 Begin to weave. Using your first color of yarn, thread the tapestry needle, and begin weaving tabby stitch from left to right, starting at the bottom left of the card. Leave a 3" (7.6 cm) tail loose at the bottom left corner. Weave across from left to right and then around to the back of the card. You will continue weaving around the card in a circle, so you end up with a seamless pouch.

07 Be sure to bubble your weft (see page 33) to ensure good, consistent tension throughout.

08 Check your work after every few rows for accuracy, and be sure to beat down the stitches with your fingers for a really tight weave (and to fit as many rows as possible)—this will ensure your bag holds its structure so you don't lose your belongings when you are on the dance floor! **(B)**

09 When you need to add a new color or piece of yarn, make sure to cross the tails of the old and new pieces over each other (see page 34). Continue weaving until you are 1" (2.5 cm) from the top of the loom.

10 Create the drawstring. Thread the tapestry needle with the end of your ribbon, leather, or cord, and weave it onto one side of the bag. Flip the loom over, and continue on the other side of the bag until you've reached the beginning. Tie the ends together in the center with overhand knots, then trim the ends.

11 Continue weaving above the drawstring with more yarn, right up to the very top of the loom. At the end, trim the yarn, leaving a 3" (7.6 cm) tail at the top.

12 Weave in the ends, including the warp tails. Don't weave the tails of the drawstrings in.

13 Using your tapestry needle, slip the loops off the spikes. Pull your pouch off the loom and turn it inside out, and gently pull the loose drawstrings through to the outside.

14 Fill your new bag up with your necessities, pull your drawstring tight, and head out for a night on the town!

RECTANGULAR LOOMS
WOVEN NECKLACE

THE THING THAT DRAWS ME (and so many others) to weaving is how the same basic steps can be interpreted in so many different ways. Depending on your personal style, this simple necklace can be left minimal and elegant, or be embellished with as many beads, fringes, and crystals as you can carry around your neck. And the fab thing is, once you've made your loom to size, it can be used over and over to create a necklace for every outfit. These one-of-a-kind pieces also make perfect gifts that can be personalized for each and every one of your friends and family.

MATERIALS

- 4" x 6" (10.2 x 15.2 cm) or postcard-sized piece of cardboard (see Note)
- Ruler
- Pencil
- Scissors
- An assortment of yarn in the colors of your choice (about half a skein), including at least one that won't stretch or break, for the warp (see page 24)
- Masking tape
- Tapestry needle
- 1 piece copper tubing, cut to match the width of the weaving
- Beads, tassels, and/or crystals, for embellishment (optional)
- 30" (76.2 cm) yarn, leather cord, or chain narrow enough to slip through the copper tube

Note: Use a piece of cardboard slightly larger than you want your pendant to be, so you have enough warp left to tie the knots that will hold the weaving in place.

01 Make your loom. Lay your cardboard piece vertically, and draw a line ½" (1.3 cm) down from, and parallel to, both short sides of the cardboard. Mark the piece every ¼" (6 mm) across both short edges. Cut these marks to the ½" (1.3 cm) line with scissors.

02 Measure and mark out how wide you want your pendant—it should be slightly smaller than the rod you are using. My sample is 3½" (8.9 cm) wide.

03 Warp the loom. Anchor the warp yarn by taping 3" (7.6 cm) of the tail to the back of the cardboard. Wrap the warp thread around the tabs you cut, starting at the bottom left of the loom and finishing at the bottom right. Check your tension every couple of rows—you want the warp to feel bouncy but not be so tight that it bends the cardboard. The finished piece will have a row of loops at the top that will hold the copper tube. (A)

04 Using your first color of yarn, thread the tapestry needle, and weave tabby stitch from left to right, starting at the bottom of the cardboard loom (keep in mind that the stitches at the bottom of your loom will appear at the top of your pendant). Be sure to bubble your weft (see page 33), to ensure good, consistent tension throughout. Check your work after every few rows for accuracy, and beat down the stitches with your fingers to cre-

ate a really tight weave—this will ensure a structure strong enough to hold any embellishments you might add later. (B)

05 When you need to add a new color or piece of yarn, make sure to cross the tails of the old and new pieces over each other (see page 34). Once you have woven about halfway up the loom (or until your pendant is as long as you desire), stop weaving, leaving about a 3" (7.6 cm) tail of yarn to weave in later. Carefully pop the bottom loops off the cardboard pegs without bending them. Thread your tube through the loops, and adjust the bottom rows of your weaving to ensure a tight fit.

06 Cut through the warp loops at the top of your loom, rotate the pendant so the cut warps are at the bottom, and tie pairs of them with overhand knots to hold your weaving in place. You can choose to leave these warp threads long, as fringe, or hide them by cutting them quite short. Weave in any loose ends on the back of the pendant.

07 If you want to add embellishments to your pendant, use thin

yarn and your tapestry needle to add beads, crystals, or tassels.

08 Thread the yarn, leather, or chain through the tube and knot the ends together.

09 Put on your fabulous woven and embellished pendant, and wait for the compliments!

A Wrap the warp threads around the tabs you cut, starting at the bottom left and finishing at the bottom right.

B Weave rows of tabby stitch beginning from the bottom left of the loom.

CIRCULAR
LOOMS

PROJECTS
IN THIS CHAPTER

AS THE NAME SUGGESTS, circular looms are the best way to create circular projects! Traditional circular looms have a round shape with teeth or pegs all the way around the outer rim. You can warp them up in two ways: either by winding the warp around both the front and back to create a "double warp," or by warping up the front only in a figure eight pattern. The trick to weaving on a circle is to ensure you weave on an odd number of warp strings. Even if you mark an odd number of notches, you will end up with an even number of warp strings, so always treat one pair of warps as one, unless you're warping from the center out as in the projects on pages 78 and 100.

· MAKING A CIRCULAR LOOM ·

There are several ways to make your own circular loom, so you don't have to purchase a manufactured one.

One of the cheapest ways is to use a sturdy paper plate or a round piece of cardboard. First, mark evenly spaced lines all around the edge. Use these marks to make cuts ⅜" (1 cm) deep around the edge. To warp your loom, thread your warp through the notches and around the "pegs," always passing the warp over the front face of the loom.

To make a small circular loom that can be displayed as is, you can use an embroidery hoop. To set up your weaving, separate the hoop pieces and use whichever hoop you like best. Wrap your warp thread once across the middle and tie it off, centering the knot in the middle of the hoop opening. Wrap more lengths of yarn so they crisscross the opening, spacing the warps evenly all around the edge, and tie each off as you did with the first. Be sure to weave on an odd number of warp strings! Unlike other loom options, you can weave into either the front or the back. For this type of loom, you can cut the warp threads off the hoop when the piece is

done, tie each into a knot, and weave the ends in, or you can leave it as-is and use the hoop to display your piece.

To make a large circular loom, you can use a Hula-hoop! As with the embroidery hoop, simply wrap the base warp around the Hula-hoop. Or, to create a circular loom with pegs that will hold your weaving in place, you can drill screws into the outer edge of the Hula-hoop at even intervals, making sure to use an odd number of screws. Then, as you would with a store-bought circular loom, wrap your warp around the screws, keeping your string to the front of the loom.

CIRCULAR LOOMS

FRINGED PLACE MATS

ALTHOUGH I DON'T EXACTLY love to cook, I do love eating and drinking with my nearest and dearest. And when I do cook, I love to set the table with candles, flowers, and lovely linens like these fringed place mats. I made my set in neutral tones and use them every time we entertain.

MATERIALS

TO MAKE 1 PLACE MAT

- 16" (40.6 cm) diameter heavyweight cardboard circle
- Ruler
- Pencil
- Scissors
- 1 small ring (I used a metal key ring)
- T-pins
- Scrap yarn
- Cotton rug warp
- Tapestry needle
- An assortment of yarn in the colors of your choice (about two skeins)
- Crochet hook, size E-4 (3.5 mm)

01 Make your loom. Mark the edge of the cardboard circle every ½" (1.3 cm). Use your scissors to cut slits at these marks, ½" (1.3 cm) deep, all around the edge.

02 Pin the small ring to the center of the loom with a T-pin. Attach four evenly spaced "anchor strings" (these can be pieces of thin scrap yarn in a different color than your warp) to the ring, to keep it in place, as follows: loop a long string into the ring, then bring the two ends to the edge of the loom and slide one on each side of a notch. Tie the string's ends into a double knot at the back of the loom. **(A)**

03 Warp the loom. Anchor the end of the warp yarn by tying it to the ring, leaving a 3" (7.6 cm) tail. Pull the long end of the warp to the edge of the cardboard loom, passing it through the first slit. Take it around the back of the tab, through the next slit to the left, and back in to the ring. Use a needle to pass the warp through the ring and back out to the next slit. If you run out of warp at any point, simply tie your first piece off on the ring, tie on a new piece, and continue warping.

04 Check your tension every couple of warps—you want the warp to

feel bouncy but not be so tight that it bends your cardboard base. Continue in this way until the entire cardboard loom is warped (you will need to tie off before the last notch to ensure an odd number of warp strings). Remove your anchor strings. (B)

05 Begin to weave. Using your first color of yarn, thread the tapestry needle and begin weaving tabby stitch from the center of the loom, around in circles. Starting close to the center ring, weave over and under two warp threads at a time. (There is not enough room at the start to go over and under every warp thread.) Make sure to bubble each finished round of tabby stitch (see page 33).

06 Once you have 2" (5.1 cm) of circular weaving completed, begin weaving over and under every warp thread. Check your work for accuracy after every few rows, and be sure to beat down the stitches to create a really tight weave—this will ensure your place mat holds its shape. When you need to add a new color or piece of yarn, make sure to cross the tails of the old and new pieces over each other

(see page 34). I alternated using gold-leafed yarn and bundles of gold thread to create the effect shown on page 78. (C)

07 Once you have woven all the way to the outer edge, carefully pop the loops off the pegs. Your place mat should hold its shape and have loops all around the outer edge.

08 Make the outer fringe using rya knots (see page 30). Cut four to seven 9" (22.9 cm) lengths of yarn per rya knot; the thicker the fiber, the fewer lengths you'll need (you will attach one rya knot per warp loop). Use your crochet hook to help you attach rya knots made from the cut yarn pieces to the loops around the edge of your place mat. Once you've attached the fringe, you can trim the ends to the desired length.

09 Invite your buddies over for a belly-warming, home-cooked meal.

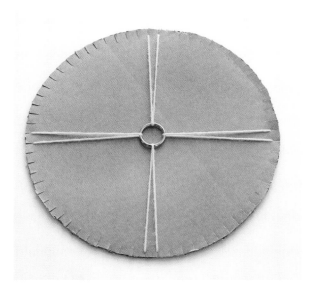

A Attach four "anchor" strings to hold a key ring to the center of the loom.

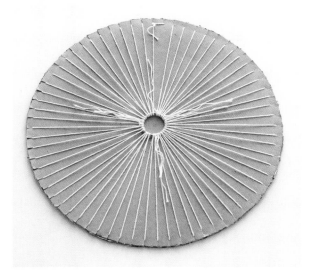

B Wrap the warp strings through the center ring and around the tabs.

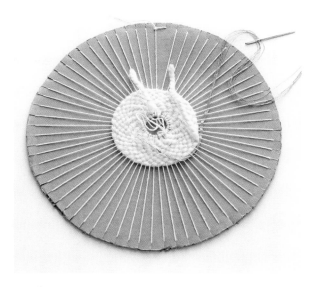

C Begin to weave from the center out, changing colors as desired.

CIRCULAR LOOMS
PLANT CRADLE

I AM A SUCKER FOR PLANTS—they add life to your living space, and I love that they clean the air. Whenever I move apartments, they're the first things I bring in. Before I had my own babies, my plants were my babies. And every baby deserves a cradle, right?

MATERIALS

- Card stock
- Plant pot
- Ruler
- Pencil
- Scissors
- Masking tape
- An assortment of yarn in the colors of your choice (about one skein), including at least one that won't stretch or break, for warping (see page 24)
- Tapestry needle
- Crochet hook, size E-4 (3.5 mm) (optional)

01 Make your loom. Cut the card stock into a 2" (5.1 cm) wide strip that measures ½" (1.3 cm) longer than the circumference of the pot's rim. Measure, mark, and cut notches ½" (1.3 cm) apart and ½" (1.3 cm) deep along one long side of the card stock.

02 Use masking tape to snugly secure the card stock around the rim of the pot, with the notches facing up. This arrangement will serve as your loom.

03 Warp the loom. Anchor the end of the warp yarn by tying it to one of the notches, leaving a 3" (7.6 cm) tail. Draw the warp thread down the outside of the pot, across the bottom, and up the other side. Draw the warp through the notch that is opposite your starting notch, around the peg to its left, and back down again. Continue all the way around the pot, wrapping every other peg until you reach your starting notch. (The warps should all neatly crisscross in the center of the bottom of the pot.) Check your tension every couple of rows—you want the warp to feel bouncy but not be so tight that it bends your card stock. (A)

04 Tie off the warp on the last notch, leaving a 3" (7.6 cm) tail.

05 Make the fringe using rya knots (see page 30). Cut four to seven 6" (15.2) lengths of yarn per rya knot; the thicker the fiber, the fewer lengths you'll need per

knot (I used 12 rya knots on my pot).

06 Flip the pot upside down and hold it between your knees. Thread the tapestry needle with your first color of yarn, and weave rows of tabby stitch, beginning at the center-bottom of the pot. Leave a 3" (7.6 cm) tail loose in the middle to weave in at the end. Because the warps are so close together where all the warp threads crisscross, you should weave over and under pairs of warp threads at first. After weaving a few rows, when the warps are more spread apart, you will be able to weave over and under every warp thread. As you need to work with an odd number of warp strings for this project, you will need to cheat and continue to treat one pair as one warp throughout the rest of your weaving.

07 Create fringe around your pot. Using your bundles of yarn from step 05, make rya knots around two warp threads at a time, using your fingers or a crochet hook. You can add the rya knots in a pattern throughout your piece like I did (I attached mine diagonally up one side of the pot as I

wove each row) but you can also add them more uniformly all the way around the bottom rim (begin to add them once you reach the bottom edge of the rim). Trim the ends to the desired length.

08 In order to lock in the rya knots, weave at least three rows of tabby stitch above the knots, alternating colors to create a pattern, if you wish. (Make sure to bubble each finished row of tabby stitch as described on page 33.)

09 Continue weaving all the way around the pot. Check your work after every few rows for accuracy, and be sure to beat down the stitches with your fingers to create a really tight weave—this will ensure your cradle holds its shape and keeps your plant safe and secure.

10 When you need to add a new color or piece of yarn, make sure to cross the tails of the old and new pieces over each other (see page 34). Continue alternating patterns of shapes, colors, and fringe until you reach the top of your pot. Using your tapestry needle, slip the loops off the notches and gently pull

the card stock loom away from your cradle.

11 Weave in the ends, using the crochet hook, and add a little plant to brighten your home.

HANG YOUR CRADLE

If you want to hang your cradle, cut four 50" (1.3 m) yarn lengths. Fold each one in half and attach each looped end with a lark's head knot (see page 31) to the plant cradle, spacing them evenly around the edge. Bring the loose ends of all four lengths of yarn together in the center, pull them taut, and tie their ends together to form the hanger.

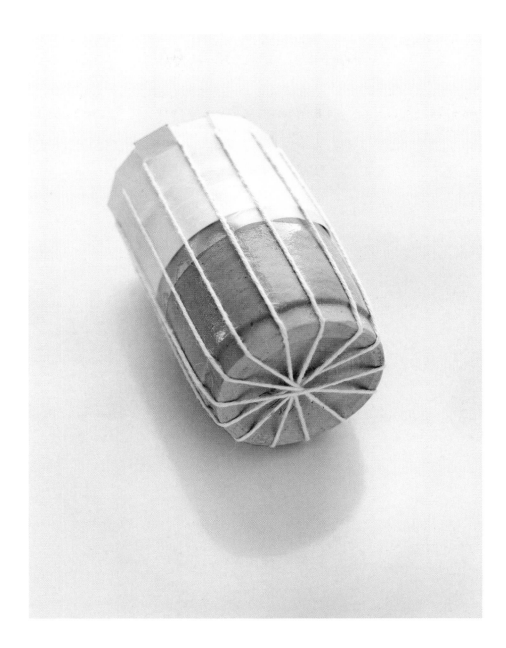

A Draw the warp thread around a tab, down the outside of the pot, across the bottom, and up the other side. Continue until the entire pot is warped.

CIRCULAR LOOMS
WRAPPED LAMPSHADE

I DON'T OWN MY OWN HOME YET, so I am all too familiar with the awful generic light fixtures that are found in most rentals—almost every house I have lived in started with awful '80s lighting. But the good thing about light fixtures is that they can be easily replaced (for me, they are always one of the first things to go). This is a great little tutorial for adding some character and personality to your home, even when it belongs to someone else.

MATERIALS

- Lampshade frame (see Resources, pages 138–139)
- An assortment of yarn in the colors of your choice (about five skeins)
- Scissors
- Lamp base or pendant light kit to fit your frame
- Beads, tassels, and/or crystals, for embellishment (optional)

01   Take a look around the room where you'll use your lampshade and note the color scheme. Do you want your lampshade to blend in with the room's décor, or stand out as a feature? If you want it to blend in, choose analogous (similar) shades of yarn. If you want it to stand out (in a good way), then choose a complementary color instead. (For a full discussion of color theory, see pages 39–41).

02   Begin to weave. Tie your first color of yarn onto one of the crossbars at the top of the lampshade frame, using a surgeon's knot (see page 35) to keep it from slipping. Slide the knot to the outer end of the cross bar. **(A)**

03   Pull the ball of yarn down to the bottom bar of the lampshade frame and wrap it around from the outside to the inside. Bring the yarn back up to the top bar and wrap it around from the outside to the inside again, creating a figure eight. **(B)**

04   Continue creating figure eights with your yarn, working your way around the frame, until the entire shade is filled in and you are happy with the way it looks. You can either use one color, or create a pattern by changing colors as you go. To change colors, use a surgeon's knot to tie your piece of yarn off onto one of the top crossbars, leaving a 2" (5.1 cm) tail. When you pick up your

A Tie your first color of yarn onto one of the crossbars using a surgeon's knot.

B Pull the ball of yarn down to the bottom bar and wrap it, creating a figure eight pattern.

next piece of yarn, tie it onto the crossbar in the same spot with another surgeon's knot and continue with your figure eights. As you wind, be sure to lay the tail of the last knot along the frame and weave it into the next section, to hide it.

05 When you have wound all the way around and completely covered the metal frame, tie the yarn off with a surgeon's knot to the nearest crossbar.

06 Embellish your creation. You can add beads, crystals, or fringe to make your piece truly custom. If you'd like to create fringe along the bottom of your shade, use lark's head knots (see page 31). Cut four to seven 6" (15.2 cm) lengths of yarn for each knot you'd like to create. The thicker the fiber, the fewer lengths you'll need for each bundle. Knot the groups to the bottom of the frame.

07 You can add beads or crystals randomly or in a neat pattern. Every time you thread one on, tie a knot directly underneath it to hold it in place. You could also slide beads on as you are winding the yarn onto the frame to integrate them into your final piece.

08 Hang your lampshade or attach it to your lamp, and fill your room with a warm glow.

CIRCULAR LOOMS
HOLIDAY ORNAMENTS

I HAVE ALWAYS LOVED THE HOLIDAYS. When I was a child, my dad would bring home a real tree, and us six kids would make tons of handmade decorations that we piled on the poor thing until you could only half tell there was a tree underneath it all.

Making ornaments is still an activity I like to do with my friends and family in the lead-up to the holidays. You can show some restraint and make only enough to adorn and enhance the beauty of your tree—or throw caution to the wind and pile them high upon every branch, like we used to do.

· ·

·MATERIALS·

- Thick cardstock or cardboard, cut into 4"–8" (10.2–20.3 cm) rounds (see Note)
- Scissors
- Ruler
- Pencil
- Assortment of yarn and embroidery floss, in the colors of your choice
- Hole punch

Note: I left my rounds plain white to let the yarn colors pop, but you can use various colors of cardstock—or even paint your cardstock—for a different look.

· ·

01 Make your circular looms. Measure, mark, and cut slits ¼" (6 mm) apart and ¼" (6 mm) deep around the edge of each cardstock round.

02 Begin to weave. Pass your first color of yarn or embroidery floss through a slit, leaving an approximately 3" (7.6 cm) knotted tail on the back side. **(A)**

03 Draw the yarn across the circle to the opposite slit, then pass it over to the back side.

04 Bring the yarn to the front by passing it through the slit to the left of the one you began on, then through the slit on the opposite side, also to the left of the previous one.

05 Keep working your way around the ornament in this way, pairing each slit with its counterpart on the opposite side of the circle, until you have gone around the entire ornament once.

A Pass your first color of yarn through a slit, leaving a knot on the back side of the round.

B Work your way around the ornament, wrapping yarn through various slits, to create a star shape.

06 Begin wrapping a second time (you may switch colors here, if you wish). This time, pair the primary slits with the slits to the left of the one opposite. Continue until you have gone around the entire ornament. **(B)**

07 Begin wrapping a third time (you may switch colors here, if you wish). This round, pair your primary slit with the slit to the right of the one opposite. Con-tinue until you have gone around the entire ornament.

08 By following the instructions here, you will create a star shape on each cardstock circle. But these ornaments can be just as beautiful if you allow yourself some freedom while you're wrapping. Instead of making a star shape like I've described, you can just pass the yarn through any slit you want to cre-ate lovely, asymmetrical shapes instead.

09 Once you are done, pull the yarn to the back of the ornament and tie a knot behind the last slit. Trim the tail.

10 Punch small holes in the tops of each ornament, so you can attach strings for hanging.

11 Admire your beautiful tree!

I ADORE THE IDEA of private spaces within other, larger spaces—a little reading nook nestled amongst cushions in a window seat, an elevated loft that you must climb a ladder to access, a pillow fort created with blankets draped over a table—they all harken back to a simpler time, when play was free and easy. This tutorial is for a special little spot that would work equally well for a pet, a child, or a quick nap for yourself. Arrange a sheepskin, a few cushions, and fairy lights, and let the outside world fade away.

MATERIALS

- 6 wooden dowels or trimmed tree branches, 6' x 1½" (183 x 3.8 cm) each
- Heavy cotton thread
- 6 wooden dowels or trimmed tree branches, 2' x 1" (60.9 x 2.5 cm) each, for the lower crosspieces and door opening
- An assortment of recycled fabric yarn (see Note)
- Scissors
- Yardstick

Note: We purchased about six skeins of recycled silk ribbon yarn for this project, but you can make your own fabric yarn from cotton sheets following the instructions on page 55 if you wish.

01 Create the teepee base (this works best if you have an extra pair of hands). Hold the six longer dowels upright. Tie them together, using the heavy cotton thread, 10" (25.4 cm) down from the top. (A)

02 Have a friend hold the bundle steady at the top while you spread the bottoms of the dowels out on the floor, 20" (50.8 cm) apart, in a large semicircle. These upright dowels will act as your loom.

03 Lash the crosspieces. While your friend continues to hold up the teepee, position one of the smaller dowels horizontally, 10" (25.4 cm) up from the bottom ends of two upright dowels and centered so that the ends of the crosspiece extend 2" (5.1 cm) beyond the upright dowels on each side. Lash the horizontal dowel to the uprights with cotton

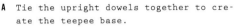

A Tie the upright dowels together to create the teepee base.

B Lash the crosspieces to the upright dowels to steady the frame.

thread in a figure eight pattern. Tie off the thread with a surgeon's knot (see page 35). **(B)**

04 Repeat the lashing process with four of the remaining dowels. The teepee frame should now stand on its own with an opening in the front. Your helper is free to go and pop the kettle on.

05 Tie the tail from a ball of the fabric yarn near the bottom of the upright dowel to the left of the opening, where the crosspiece is lashed to it.

06 Draw the ball of yarn over the next upright dowel to the left. Wind it around the upright, from the outside to the inside (clock-

wise). Continue yarn-winding each of the upright dowels, all the way around to the last dowel on the other side of the opening. Now reverse the direction of your winding, working your way back to the opening on the other side, still wrapping dowels from outside to inside. When you finish one ball of fabric yarn, tie it

C Wind the fabric yarn around each dowel
from the outside to the inside all the
way up the base.

off and tie on the tail of a new ball. (C)

07 Continue wrapping the fabric yarn onto the upright dowels. When the weft yarns are 1' (30.5 cm) from where the uprights meet, wrap the fabric yarn all the way around, until you reach the lashing. Tie off the fabric yarn.

08 Decorate the last small dowel with lark's head knots (see page 31) of fabric yarn and silk strips in varying lengths and lash it over the door opening. Or use some of your excess yarn to personalize the teepee in other ways. Try a few flags popping out from the top, some bunting over the door, or peace signs and triangles tacked onto the bottom—the opportunities are bounded only by your imagination. Then find the right corner of the room for your new private space. This structure could work, temporarily, just as well outdoors as it does indoors. It's really quite light and portable, so you can cart it around to chase a spot of sunshine, or the quiet.

CIRCULAR LOOMS
DREAM CATCHER

Before I had children, I used to sleep like a lamb. Not only did I fall asleep in a snap, but I stayed asleep all night and awoke to find my covers as they were made the morning before. I could catch some Zs on a park bench under a magazine. Fall asleep at the cinema watching an action movie. Sneak forty winks standing up on a train. And when I awoke, I would stretch languorously, have no recollection of dreams, and blissfully continue with my day.

But now I am the hyper-attentive mother bear of a brood of defenseless babes. I am the last to bed in the evening. Then I toss and I turn. I entertain raucous dreams. I wake quickly to any creak in the floorboards or mattress springs from the next room. I sleep no more.

So I created this dream catcher to help soothe my mind, lull me to sleep, and bring me good dreams. At the very least, it's something pretty to look at while sleep evades me.

MATERIALS

- 2 metal macramé rings, 10" (25 cm) and 3" (7.6 cm) in diameter
- Assorted yarns in the colors of your choice (about two skeins)
- Decorative items, such as beads and feathers (optional)
- Scissors
- Tapestry needle

01 Prepare the rings. Choose your first color of yarn; this will be the main color of your piece. Hold the tail of the yarn to the larger ring with your thumb, and wrap the yarn around the ring. Be sure to keep your winding very tight so that there are no gaps. Covering each ring in yarn will keep the woven yarn from slipping off the smooth metal in step 04.

02 You can either cover the entire ring in one color or make a pattern by changing colors. To

change colors (or if you run out of yarn), leave a 6" (15.2 cm) tail. Lay the tail of the new color along the hoop in the path of your first color. Wind the first color of yarn over the larger ring until it runs out, and then simply wind the new color of yarn over top of it. Continue wrapping until the entire ring is covered in yarn. Cut the yarn from the skein, leaving a length of about 4' (1.2 m) as a tail.

03   Repeat steps 01 and 02 with the smaller ring.

04   Place both rings on a flat surface, with the smaller ring inside the larger one. Take the tail from the larger ring and slide it up through the center of the smaller ring and back around the top of the larger ring in a figure-eight pattern. (A) Continue all the way around the larger ring to attach and hold the smaller ring in place. (B)

05   Repeat with the tail from the smaller ring and tie off. (C) I used cream-colored yarn for both rings at right, but they look great when they're wrapped in contrasting colors as on page 96.

06   Create the fringe. I like to use two layers of fringe—one for the smaller ring and one for the larger one. For the larger ring's fringe, cut one hundred 26" (66 cm) lengths of yarn, to create twenty lark's head knots (see page 31) made with five yarn pieces each. (You can modify this based on your preference and on the thickness of your yarn.) Vary your colors here if you choose.

07   For the smaller ring's fringe, cut fifty 26" (66 cm) lengths of yarn, to create ten lark's head knots made of five yarn pieces each. Instead of yarn, I used several lengths of gold thread to create my knots.

08   Tie on the twenty larger ring's lark's head knots in the bottom third of the larger ring. Make sure not to overlap them or leave any gaps between the knots.

09   Use lark's head knots to attach the ten smaller ring's bundles. Trim the bottom of the fringe to the length you desire.

10   If you are adding beads, thread them through the ends of the tassels and secure them there with overhand knots. To keep the piece weighted evenly, push larger beads higher up, toward the center, and place smaller beads at or near the ends.

11   If you want to add a feather to a tassel, lay a tail alongside the feather's quill, wind yarn around it, and tie the yarn off with an overhand knot. Trim. Use larger feathers in the center and smaller ones toward the edge.

12   Create a hanger (optional—you can also hang it directly on a nail, as I did here). Attach a short piece of yarn to the center top of the large ring with a lark's head knot. Tie an overhand knot with the tails to create a loop.

13   Take a little nap under your new dream catcher!

A Lay both rings on a flat surface and use the tail from the larger ring to begin attaching the smaller ring.

B Using a figure-eight pattern, wrap the yarn around both rings until the smaller ring is secure.

C Repeat with the tail from the smaller ring and tie off.

CIRCULAR LOOMS
RYA KNOT CUSHION

I SIT FOR HOURS AT A TIME when I'm in the weaving zone, so a comfortable perch is essential. I like to sit on a stool because it gives me the best posture, but it can still become a little uncomfortable after I've been in the same position for a long time. This cute rya knotted cover does just the trick—it cushions the stool just the right amount and is removable, so it can be swapped in and out to match your décor.

MATERIALS

- Assorted yarn in the colors of your choice (about five skeins)
- Small, inexpensive stool (see Resources, pages 138–139)
- Piece of cardboard slightly larger than the stool seat
- Pencil
- Ruler
- Scissors
- Cotton rug warp
- Masking tape
- Tapestry needle

01 Prepare your yarn. This cushion top is made by attaching rya knots of varying lengths (see page 30) to a circular cardboard loom to create a fringe. The number of yarn pieces you need per knot depends on the thickness of your yarn (the thicker the yarn, the fewer pieces needed for each knot). With a medium-weight yarn, use eight lengths of yarn per knot for the cushion: Cut 1,600 pieces, each 4" (10.2 cm) long, in an assortment of yarns, to create 200 rya knot bundles. For the knots for the outer fringe, cut 400 pieces of yarn, each 8" (20.3 cm) long, for 20 knots with 20 yarn pieces each.

02 Make your loom. Draw and cut out a cardboard circle that measures 1" (2.5 cm) larger in diameter than the stool top. Measure, mark, and cut an odd number of slits, ½" (1.3 cm) apart and ½" (1.3 cm) deep, all around the edge of your cardboard circle.

03 Poke a small hole in the center of the cardboard loom with your scissors.

04 Warp the loom. You will be warping it from the center out. Poke a 3" (7.6 cm) tail of the cotton rug warp through the hole and tape it down on the back side.

05 Turn the loom over to the front side. Pull the warp yarn from the center to the edge of the disc, and pass it through a slit. Loop the thread around the "peg" to the

left, then draw the yarn across the front of the disk, around the peg on the opposite side, wrapping to the left, to complete that loop. Continue warping the loom, moving to the peg to the left and drawing the yarn across the front of the disk until every peg is wrapped. **(A)** Check your tension every couple of wraps—you want the warp to feel bouncy but not be so tight that it bends the cardboard.

06 Begin to weave. Thread your tapestry needle with a piece of yarn cut to two arm's lengths. As you did for the warp, draw the yarn through the hole in the center from back to front, leaving a 3" (7.6 cm) tail. Using basic tabby stitch, weave over and under pairs of warp threads. (At this point, there isn't enough room to go over and under every single thread.)

07 Once you've woven about 1" (2.5 cm), start weaving over and under each warp thread. Check your work after every few rows. Be sure to beat down the stitches with your fingers (see page 33) to create a really tight weave—this will ensure your stool cushion holds its shape. Continue

weaving until you have 2" (5.1 cm) of tabby stitch.

08 Use your short lengths of yarn to add a round of rya knots to the weaving. **(B)** After one round, weave another 1" (2.5 cm) of tabby stitch to lock them in. Be sure to beat down the rows with your fingers to keep the weaving packed in tight. **(C)**

09 Repeat this pattern until you are 1" (2.5 cm) from the edge of the loom. Add a row of rya-knot fringe with the longer yarn pieces, then continue weaving tabby stitch until you reach the edge of the loom.

10 Pop the loops off the cardboard loom. If your weaving has been nice and tight, the pompom cushion will hold its shape.

11 Using your tapestry needle, weave in any ends and trim them short.

12 Lay your cushion on the floor face down and center the stool upside down on top of it. Thread the tapestry needle with the cotton rug warp and tie it to one of the outer loops you popped off of the loom, leaving a 10"

(25.4 cm) tail. Draw the warp thread across the underside of the stool seat and through the loop on the opposite side. Pull the warp thread back across the underside of the seat to the loop to the left of your first loop, then back across, to the opposite loop that is to the right of the previous loop.

13 Pull the cotton warp thread tight as you cross and recross the circle, attaching it to the stool seat. Continue until you have passed through every loop, then tie the end of the thread to the 10" (25.4 cm) tail you left at the beginning. **(D)**

14 Turn over your stool and marvel at its cushiness.

A Warp the cardboard disc from the center out, looping the cotton rug warp around opposite pegs until every peg is wrapped.

B Weave about 2" (5.1 cm) of tabby stitch, then begin creating rya knots with the 4" (10 cm) lengths of yarn.

C After each round of rya knots, weave 1" (2.5 cm) of tabby stitch to lock them in.

D Attach the cushion to the stool by tying cotton rug warp to the outer loops, crossing and recrossing the stool base.

CIRCULAR LOOMS
DENIM CATCHALL BASKET

BASKETS ARE MY THING. They give my houseplants stylish homes, I organize my kids' toys in them, I pile blankets and cushions in them when I'm not snuggling on the couch—they are such a clever way to keep everything in order and looking good. I love to buy vintage baskets from thrift stores and flea markets, but making your own can add a personal touch to your space. This basket can be made in different sizes for a variety of purposes, but this tutorial makes one medium-sized basket.

MATERIALS

- 4 pairs of old denim jeans (preferably with little to no stretch)
- Ruler
- Pen or tailor's chalk
- Scissors
- Masking tape
- Large pot or bucket, for shaping
- Crochet hook, size E-4 (3.5 mm)
- Needle and thread to match the fabric

01 Create the denim strips. Using your ruler and pen or tailor's chalk, draw 1" (2.5 cm) marks along the inner and outer legs of the front and back of three of your four pairs of old jeans. If you can, get jeans of slightly different washes—this can create a good element of interest to your basket (white denim and really light washes can look totally stylish and chic when layered together with darker denim).

02 With the pants face up on a table or flat surface, place your ruler at a slight angle high on the outer upper thigh, right near the pocket. Line up the first outer mark with one that is 1" (2.5 cm) lower on the inside leg, and draw a diagonal line to connect the two marks.

03 Move your ruler to the next mark on the outer leg, just below the first mark, and line it up with the next lower mark on the inner leg. Draw a diagonal line to join them. Continue in this manner all the way down the length of each leg of your jeans. (A)

04 Turn the jeans over so that the back side faces up, and this time, place your ruler straight across the first two marks at the top of one leg (rather than on an angle).

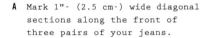

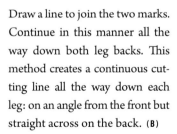

A Mark 1"- (2.5 cm-) wide diagonal sections along the front of three pairs of your jeans.

B Flip the jeans over, and mark 1"- (2.5 cm-) wide horizontal sections along the back.

C Cut through a single layer of fabric on both sides of the jeans, following the marked lines, to create one continuous piece of denim "ribbon."

Draw a line to join the two marks. Continue in this manner all the way down both leg backs. This method creates a continuous cutting line all the way down each leg: on an angle from the front but straight across on the back. **(B)**

05 Cut the first denim strip. Use the scissors to poke a hole from the front into the outside seam, beginning at the first line you drew. Cut only the top layer, and when you reach the end of the first diagonal line at the outer seam, turn the jeans over, and

follow the straight line across the back. Flip the jeans and follow each line until you reach the bottom of the first leg. This method creates one continuous piece of denim "ribbon."

06 Repeat the process for rest of the legs of the marked jeans **(C)**. Cut the larger strips into three 1" (2.5 cm) strips each, for a total of 18 long pieces of ribbon. **(D)** Put them to the side.

07 Cut the legs off the last pair of jeans, just below the crotch.

08 Use your ruler and pencil to measure out and mark vertical strips that are 1" (2.5 cm) wide on the jean legs.

09 Cut the strips. You should end up with eight to ten strips that are each approximately 30" (76.2 cm) long, depending on the jeans' original inseam measurement. These vertical strips will be used for your warp.

10 Gather the warp strips and hold them at their centers. Turn the container upside down and lay the

D Cut the larger strips into three strips each, following the marked lines.

E Spread the warp strips out in a radiating pattern on the bottom of your container.

F Weave tabby stitch into the warp strips with the longer denim ribbon.

bundle out on the flat bottom of your container. Spread the strips out in a radiating pattern so that they hang down the container's sides. Use masking tape to hold the strips in place so that they stay flat and evenly spaced. (E)

11 Tuck one of your longer denim ribbons into the center of the warp strips, leaving a 3" (7.6 cm) tail. With the other end of the ribbon, weave tabby stitch over and under the warp strips, as close to the center as possible. Try to keep all of the strips flat.

(F) Continue weaving until you have a base that is comparable in diameter to the base of the container. Check your work after every few rows. Your strips should not twist or crisscross. When you finish a ribbon and need to add another, overlap the tails of the old and new pieces, and carry on weaving in the same direction. You can stitch the strips in place, if you wish, to create a more secure bond.

12 Once your base is the correct size, weave around the outside of

the container until you have 3" (7.6 cm) of warp strips left.

13 Use your crochet hook to vertically weave the remaining length of your last denim ribbon into the basket. Undo the masking tape, and repeat the weaving-in with all of the warp ends.

14 Hand-stitch any stray strips in place securely with the needle and thread.

15 Fill your new basket with treasures and store it within arm's reach.

NON
TRADITIONAL
LOOMS

PROJECTS
IN THIS CHAPTER

PEOPLE OF MANY CULTURES have been weaving for many thousands of years, but it's only been relatively recently that weaving's resurgence has made it easy to just pop down to the local craft store and pick up a loom or ready-made yarn and supplies. In the past—and even now, in many cultures—weavers had to be more creative in coming up with ways to create woven projects. In Central America, backstrap weavers use their bodies as looms. People in Ghana weave with natural elements that are readily available, like coconut fronds.

Modern artists often draw from the natural and non-standard methods of the past to create unique and contemporary projects. Artist Sheila Hicks has woven large projects on an upturned table. Artist and master weaver Fran James made a name for herself by gathering and processing most of the materials for her work from the natural surroundings of her homeland; she was known for weaving organic elements like strips of cedar bark into baskets. This chapter explores some non-traditional looms and materials that I've used in my work. Use them as a jumping off point to explore and to create one-of-a-kind pieces for your life and home.

FINDING

NON-TRADITIONAL LOOMS AND MATERIALS

Opportunities to weave and create art are everywhere. A walk through nature, a spring clean of your home, or helping a friend or relative sort through mementos can stir up ideas and opportunities to create meaningful projects. Many things can be made into a loom—as long as you can create a frame out of it, you can weave on it. Your grandmother's paintbrushes could be lashed together to create a loom for a personal project. Weaving into a well-worn seat of a chair passed down through your family could give new life to an heirloom. Shells, seaweed, and seagrasses collected on a beloved vacation could be used to create an ephemeral beach weaving to be photographed and washed back into the sea at the next high tide. Once you open your eyes, you will find many objects in your everyday life and immediate surroundings are just begging to be changed, improved, and embellished with your new weaving skills.

DRAPED WALL HANGING

I LOVE TO CREATE TEXTURAL HANGINGS for my home. Making art from fiber (especially repurposed fiber) is a simple way to add interest and originality to a space without spending a lot of money. Plus, it's easy to create a custom size to match your personal space, whether you want to fill a wall above a couch, a bed, or a funny-shaped space between bookcases.

. . . .

MATERIALS

- Variety of fibers in a light tonal range, including yarn, fabric strips, T-shirt yarn, and muslin (about 10–12 skeins, see Note)
- Scissors
- 2 S hooks (optional)
- Rolling clothes rack (optional)
- Wooden dowel of the desired length, 1.5" (3.8 cm) diameter
- Nails or other hanging hardware

Note: As with most of my projects, this one does not require you to spend a lot of money. These are the materials I used in the hanging shown here, but you can improvise with scraps of whatever you already have in your stash if you prefer.

. . . .

01 Prepare your fibers. Cut them into a variety of lengths to create visual interest in the final piece. The exact lengths will depend on the space your hanging will occupy, but a good general rule is anywhere from 2'–7' (61–213.4 cm) per fiber (keeping in mind that each piece will be half the length once folded over the dowel). It's best if you cut each type of fiber to the same length, so you can group them together; for example: three pieces of sari silk, each 6' (183 cm) long; four pieces of a variety of thick and thin yarns, each 5' (152.4 cm) long; and six pieces of fabric strips or T-shirt yarn, each 7' (213.4 cm) long. You may need more to fill out your hanging, depending on the space you're filling, but this would be a good start.

02 Prepare your workspace. If using, attach the S hooks, oriented in opposite directions, at either end of the clothes rack. Place the dowel in the cradle of the hooks. Alternatively, you can lay your piece flat on a large, clean surface (like the floor) and work from there.

03 Create the hanging. Select one group of your fibers and tie it at one end of the dowel using a lark's head knot (see page 31). Don't try to line the ends up—this piece looks best when it's more loose and organic.

04 Select another group and tie it onto the dowel using a lark's head knot. This time, braid half of the group and leave the rest hanging.

05 Select another group and tie it onto the dowel using a lark's head knot. This time, tie overhand knots randomly along the length of the fiber.

06 Continue adding groupings of fibers all the way across the dowel, either in the same order as steps 03 through 05, or creating your own arrangement. In the hanging pictured, I included tassels (see page 32), pompoms, braids, and knots of varying thicknesses to add texture.

07 Once the dowel is full, cut a 12" (30.5 cm) length of fiber of any kind. Weave a small section near the top, using four or five loose fibers in a group as a sort of warp. Weave four or five pass-

A Weave small sections throughout the hanging, using groupings of loose fibers as a sort of warp.

es with your fingers, then tie the weft fibers off—or leave the tails hanging, as part of the design. Continue to weave small sections throughout your piece. The aim is to make it look random, so just weave a few small sections here and there throughout the hanging. **(A)**

08 When you are happy with your design, hang it on your wall. I hung mine from hooks, but you can also just balance the dowel on two nails at either end. At this point, you may want to trim some sections, or add or subtract certain elements, to create harmony in your design.

I LOVE MORNING BIKE RIDES around the neighborhood during the fall. The crisp smell in the air, the chilly breeze, and seeing everyone in their autumn garb—it all helps me welcome the change in season. During one ride, I dreamed up a fun fiber project: to spruce up my old, worn bike basket. I wanted to use elements that always inspire my weavings—bright colors, wild textures, the aesthetics of the 1970s—in this piece. Since the wires of the basket offer a natural grid to weave into, it was the perfect structure to go a bit wild with the design.

NON-TRADITIONAL LOOMS
BICYCLE BASKET

MATERIALS

- Wire bicycle basket
- An assortment of yarn in the colors of your choice (about two skeins, see Note)
- Scissors
- Embellishments, such as bells or flowers (optional)

Note: I used pima cotton thread for the feathery tassels, and kinky yarn for the weaving. Thicker or more textured yarn will fill out the space between the basket wires best.

01 Prepare the yarn. Each fringe piece will be made from bundles of long strips of yarn in the colors of your choice. To make the yarn strips a uniform length, choose an item to wrap your yarn around, like a small book that's as long as you'd like the fringe to be—I made mine the height of the basket. Hold the tail of the yarn at one end of the book, and wrap it around the book many times. (The more wraps, the fatter and fluffier your fringe will be.) Use your scissors to cut through all the wrapped yarn at one end of the book. Repeat this process until you have created fifty or so bundles. Set them aside.

02 Begin to weave, using the basket's wire grid as the warp, and make several rows of tabby stitch onto it. To begin, use a tight double knot to tie the end of the yarn onto the bottom left vertical wire on the front of the basket. (A)

03 Using your fingers, weave tabby stitch across the basket front. Bring the yarn over the next

A Tie the end of the yarn to the bottom left vertical wire on the front of the basket.

B Weave tabby stitch across the basket front, using the basket wires as your warp.

vertical wire, then under the one after that, and so on, from left to right, until you reach the end of the row. Repeat the weaving for the next row, this time working right to left and alternating the pattern of over-and-under, working your way all the way across. **(B)**

04 When you reach the end of your first piece of yarn, cross its tail over the tail of your next one, and continue weaving. When

you reach the central horizontal basket wire, you're ready to start adding your first row of fringe! Using a handful of the bundles you set aside, attach lark's head knots (see page 31) all the way across the wire, then trim them short.

05 Continue weaving tabby stitch on the rest of the basket front until you reach the top. Tie off the last of your weaving with an overhand knot.

06 Attach your remaining bundles to the top vertical wire of both sides of the basket and around the two front corners using lark's head knots, to create a fringe that will flutter along as you ride in style.

07 Lend your personality and originality to the basket by alternating the lengths of the fringe or adding embellishments, like bells and flowers, to your design.

NON-TRADITIONAL LOOMS
BRANCH WEAVING

I RECENTLY WENT AWAY to a retreat in New Hampshire, and being in that natural environment inspired me to make some little treasures with my forest finds. This is a project that can just as easily be done in a canoe on a lake as it can at an inner-city park. All you need is a forked branch, some yarn, and a warm summer afternoon.

I like to make these as keepsakes, and I display them on tables as a reminder of my time in nature. You can also create a delicate wall arrangement by hanging them on hooks in small groupings.

. MATERIALS .

- A forked branch
- Assorted yarn in the colors of your choice (about one skein), including at least one that won't stretch or break, for warping (see page 24)
- Scissors
- Tapestry needle

01 Take a stroll in nature. Choose a forked branch that speaks to you—one that feels good in your hands. It's best to find one that has a rough texture, as this will help hold the warp threads in place.

02 Warp the loom. Turn your branch sideways so that the open forked end is facing right. Anchor the end of the warp yarn by tying it onto the upper tine of the fork, 2" (5.1 cm) in from the V in the fork. This yarn will run in a vertical figure eight between the two tines and will serve as a base for you to weave into.

03 Next, run your warp yarn under the bottom tine and back up to the top, about ½" (1.3 cm) from that first knot. Continue the figure-eight pattern across the two tines of the forked part of the branch. Check your tension every couple of rows—you want the warp to be bouncy but not so tight that it pulls your branches out of their natural position. When the wrapping is 2" (5.1 cm) from the tips of the forked branches, secure the warp with a surgeon's knot (see page 35). Trim any excess warp thread. If your branch is slippery, you can secure your warp by wrapping the branches as you wind the figure-eight, as I have. (A)

04 Begin to weave. Using your first color of yarn, cut two pieces of yarn as long as your fingertip-to-

A Anchor the warp yarn, and warp the
branch in a figure-eight pattern.

fingertip wingspan. With your branch opening still facing right, thread the tapestry needle, and weave tabby stitch from the bottom up, starting at the bottom right edge (the edge farthest from the V). Be sure to bubble your weft (see page 33) to ensure that you have good, consistent tension throughout your weaving. Check your work after every few rows. Be sure to beat down the stitches with your fingers to create a really tight weave—this will ensure your weaving holds its shape.

05   When you need to add a new color or piece of yarn, make sure to cross the tails of the old and new pieces over each other (see page 34). As your weaving gets closer to the V, it will become more difficult to weave into each warp. Skip warp threads as needed until you have filled all of the spaces between the warps.

06   Weave in the ends.

07   Find a special place to display your nature-inspired piece!

NON-TRADITIONAL LOOMS
FESTIVAL HAIR TAPESTRY

I HAVE A VINTAGE WEAVING BOOK called *Weaving Is for Everybody*. On the cover is a photo of a mom and her kids weaving—the little ones look like they are into it, but her teenage daughter does not look impressed. I think if the mom had had this hair-tapestry project on hand, she would have won her over and gotten a much nicer cover for the book. Hindsight is 20/20, right?

MATERIALS

- Willing participant with longer hair, or a clip-in hair extension
- Washi tape (optional)
- Wide-tooth comb
- Embroidery floss or thin cotton yarn, in the color of your choice
- Tapestry needle

01 Comb through a section of hair that is 2" (5.1 cm) wide. Alternatively, if you're using a hair clip, use washi tape to attach the top of the clip to a smooth, flat surface.

02 Set the comb's teeth at the bottom of the section of hair you want to weave into. The comb creates sections of hair that act as the warp. You will be weaving from top to bottom, toward the comb. (A)

03 Thread the needle with the embroidery thread or cotton yarn. Use it to weave tabby stitch from left to right, starting at the top of the section of hair. Use your left hand to hold the comb in place as you weave with your right.

04 Create a second row underneath the first, being sure to go over the opposite "warp threads."

05 Check your work every few rows. Be sure to beat down the stitches with your fingers (see page 33), to ensure consistent rows.

06 When you finish a color, or want to add a new piece of yarn, cross the tails of the two pieces over each other (page 34). Lay the new piece behind the warp thread where the old one ended, then carry on weaving in the same direction. Weave at least 2" (5.1 cm).

A Set the comb's teeth at the bottom of the hair you are weaving into to create "warps."

07 When you are happy with your design, you can weave in the ends. Thread each tail and work it back in vertically, over and under the warps immediately above or below it.

08 Once you have finished weaving the ends in, style the hair to really show off the featured tapestry. We added some tassels (see page 32), for a bohemian look.

09 Time to go dance!

NON-TRADITIONAL LOOMS
CRYSTAL MAT

OVER THE YEARS, I have collected lots of little treasures. I used to keep them in a jewelry box hidden from pirates and wee hands. But recently I realized that I gain more pleasure from creating special spaces for them, so I can always have them on display, close enough to pick up.

This mat can be used for any of your cherished treasures, from crystals to plants to loose jewelry. This version sits nicely on a table or shelf, but it can easily be hung, too.

MATERIALS

- Two 6" (15.2 cm) bamboo skewers
- Scissors
- Ruler
- White glue
- An assortment of yarn (about one skein), in the colors of your choice
- Tapestry needle

01 Make your loom. Using your scissors, snip the pointy ends off the skewers. Use your ruler to find the middle of each skewer, then create a notch with your scissors. Measuring from the center out, mark smaller notches with your scissors every ½" (1.3 cm) along the full length of each skewer.

02 Apply a small dot of glue to the center notch of both skewers and let it dry until it's tacky. Cross one skewer on top of the other at the glued notch. Allow to dry completely.

03 Begin to weave. Lay a 1" (2.5 cm) tail of your first color of yarn along one of the skewers. Holding the loom like an X, wrap the yarn around the junction of the skewers from top to bottom three times. Then wind from left to right three times.

04 Still holding the loom in the X position, wind the yarn around the top left skewer over, under, and back over. (A+B)

05 Pull the yarn down and do the same to the bottom left skewer. Carry on, moving around the cross clockwise, wrapping each skewer as you go. Take care not to let any of the strands overlap when winding, and use your fingernails to space threads evenly.

A Holding the loom in the X position, wind the yarn around each skewer to create the weaving.

B Wind the yarn around each skewer over, under, and back over before moving on to the next skewer.

The notches will keep the yarn from slipping in toward the center and keep the pattern even. After winding 1" (2.5 cm) and reaching the second notch, you can choose to change color or pattern.

To change color, leave a 1" (2.5 cm) tail of the original color and twist it together with 1" (2.5 cm) of the new color. Lay this tail along the skewer and be sure to cover it every time you make another round. You can trim the tails once the two pieces are securely overlapped. To change pattern, the next time you come to a new skewer, pass the yarn under then over and back under before moving on to the next skewer.

06 Continue all the way around the loom until you reach the last ½" (1.3 cm)—you should have one notch left on the skewers.

07 Cut a 1" (1.3 cm) long tail and thread it through the tapestry needle. Weave in the end by tucking it in between the wrapped stick and the weaving on the back side.

08 Create fringe. I like to use a con-trasting color to really make my mat pop. You will tie these on in groups, so the total number you cut will depend on the thickness of your yarn. I used two hundred 6" (15.2 cm) lengths of yarn (50 groups of four). Consider the colors you use—you can make a pattern with your color choices here.

09 Beginning on the outermost thread of your mat, tie on a group of four pieces of yarn with lark's head knots (see page 31).

10 Continue attaching fringe with lark's heads knots all the way along the outer edge of your mat, being sure not to leave any gaps between knots. Take care that the knots are close to one another without overlapping. Trim the bottom of the fringe to even out the ends.

11 Lay your mat on a table with the fringe combed out, and place your precious items on top.

HANG YOUR MAT

If you want to hang your mat, cut four 50" (1.3 m) yarn pieces in a color of your choice. Fold each one in half and use a lark's head knot to attach it to a corner of the mat. Do the same for the other three corners. Tie the loose ends together over the center of the mat. Hang from a hook on your wall.

NON-TRADITIONAL LOOMS
NATURE WEAVING

I ALWAYS FEEL AS IF I've pushed the reset button after a jaunt in the wild (and not-so-wild), and one of my favorite outdoor activities is treasure-hunting for precious objects: smooth acorns, rainbow-colored leaves, a bird's egg, or perfectly weathered driftwood. This tutorial is a simple one that can be completed after an adventure in the great outdoors, and it is a great way to bring the magic of nature back to the comfort of your home.

. . . .

MATERIALS

- 12" x 16" (30.5 x 40.6 cm) rectangular loom
- Cotton rug warp
- Scissors
- Treasures from nature (see Note)
- Toothpicks
- Epoxy resin
- Stick or dowel, for hanging
- Drill and drill bit (optional)

Note: Gather together a collection of objects that are all about the same length: leaves, seed pods, vines, feathers, flowers, bark, or twigs. I used long grass for this project and added stone and wood beads to a long, dramatic fringe.

. . . .

01 Warp the loom. Tie the tail of the cotton rug warp to the bottom left-hand corner of the frame with a surgical knot (see page 35). Bring the warp up and around the left-hand top peg, then back down and around the second left-hand bottom peg. Finish all the warping in this manner, working from left to right. Check the warp tension every couple of rows—you want it to be bouncy but not so tight that the fibers are strained and stiff. When the warp is at least as wide as one of your natural treasures, tie the warp fiber off with a surgical knot.

02 Prepare your treasures for weaving. I used long grasses and wove each piece horizontally through the warp, just as if it were a weft fiber.

03 Add natural materials into the

A Attach natural treasures to your fringe
using overhand knots.

weaving from the top down: You can plan their placement strategically by laying them out beforehand in a symmetrical and balanced arrangement, or you can just weave them into the warp fibers freestyle, allowing the materials to organically dictate the flow of the piece as you go. Carefully tuck the object in over and under the warp fibers until the entire object is secure.

04   To add another found object directly above or below the first, be sure to tuck it into the warp threads so it alternates with the first one. This creates a sort of net, or tension, between the two pieces and holds them both more securely in place. Stop the weaving when it's 14" (35.6 cm) tall. You'll use the rest of the warp threads to create the fringe at the bottom of the piece.

05   When you have finished incorporating all of the objects you desire, turn the loom over.

06   Using a toothpick, dot the resin wherever a warp thread touches a natural treasure. This will hold your weaving in place when you take it off the loom. Allow the resin to dry, following the instructions on the package.

07   Slip the weaving off the loom pegs and thread the stick or dowel through the loops at the top of your weaving. Cut the long bottom loops of unused warp, creating a fringe. Tie pairs of the warp threads snugly up against the bottom row of the weaving with overhand knots and add in more lengths of cotton rug warp to create the long fringe shown here.

08   If you'd like to hang some treasures from the fringe, wrap and knot them randomly into the fringe. You can use the drill to make holes in larger items like shells and attach them with an overhand knot to a portion of your fringe or to the bottom of your piece with extra lengths of rug warp. (A)

NON-TRADITIONAL LOOMS
CAMERA STRAP

SMARTPHONES AND PHOTOS have become ubiquitous, but there is something special about taking "real" photos with a camera. We are always lugging about so many *essential* items from place to place—my pockets are always full, my bags are always overflowing, and my hands are usually holding at least one tiny grubby mitt—so it's nice to be able to just pop something around your neck and forget about it. Although this tutorial is for a camera strap, the same instructions could also be used for a belt, guitar strap, or even a dog leash.

MATERIALS

- Measuring tape
- Cotton rug warp
- Scissors
- Masking tape
- 4 straight drinking straws (I used metal straws, but plastic would work just fine)
- An assortment of yarn in the colors of your choice (about one skein)

01 Wrap the measuring tape around your neck to determine the length of your camera strap. Note the size, and cut four lengths of cotton rug warp 10" (25.4 cm) longer than the intended length of your strap.

02 Tie the four lengths together at one end using an overhand knot, leaving a 5" (12.7 cm) tail above the knot. The lengths of warp below the knot will be much longer. Using the masking tape, tape the knot to a table or stable surface.

03 Thread each of the longer warp fibers onto a drinking straw.

Slide the straws all the way up to the top of the warp strands, near the knot.

04 Begin to weave. Tie your first color of weft yarn onto the left-most warp, just above the drinking straw. Weave it over and under the straws from left to right, using your fingers to keep the fiber on the straws. (A)

05 Weave the second row directly underneath the first, from right to left, making sure to pass your yarn over and under the straws opposite to the previous row. Continue the weaving in this way, until most of the straws

have been covered. Check your work every few rows. Be sure to beat down the stitches (see page 33) with your fingers, to create a really tight weave—this will ensure that your strap will hold its shape. However, don't weave too tightly. You want the stitches to be sturdy, but not so tight that they squash plastic straws or can't be easily shifted down later.

06 When you finish a color, or want to add a new piece of yarn, be sure to allow the ends of the old and new weft fibers to overlap. Lay the tail of your new weft behind the warp thread where the original one ended, and carry on weaving in the same direction.

07 The straws won't be long enough for the entire length of the piece. Once you've woven enough that the straws are nearly covered, shift them down, away from the weaving, so that the straws are exposed again. Continue on in this manner, weaving a few rows then pulling the straws down, until you are 5" (12.7 cm) from the ends.

08 Slide the straws completely off the warps. Tie the rug warps

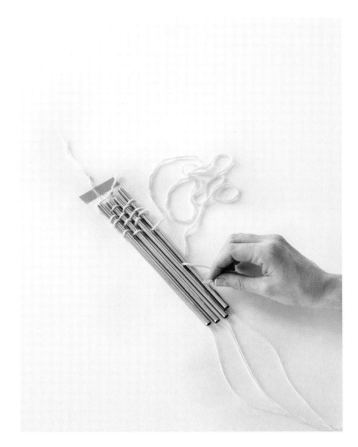

A Thread each warp through a straw, and weave over and under the straws from left to right.

together in an overhand knot to keep your weaving in place.

09 You can attach a camera to the ends by tying the loose warp ends through the holes on the sides of the camera.

10 At this point, you can add little tassels to the ends of your strap like we did, if you wish (see page 32). Attach as many or few as you like!

NON-TRADITIONAL LOOMS
WOVEN PARTY BACKDROP

NOTHING BEATS A CELEBRATION in the great outdoors when the weather is fine. Whether it's a wedding, a birthday, or simply a picnic get-together with friends, you can add a little special thought to your affair by creating a backdrop as part of your decorations—use it as a great photo backdrop or a beautiful way to help guests find your event. I created this all-weather hanging between two birch branches, but you could weave the design between two trees if you're partying al fresco!

MATERIALS

- An assortment of thick yarn or recycled fabric strips in the colors of your choice (see Note)
- Two 6' (1.8 m) birch branches, cleanly trimmed
- Two medium-sized buckets
- Bag of sand

Note: We used two skeins of recycled chiffon ribbon and one skein of wool yarn. If you'd like to make your own fabric yarn, you can use any kind of clothing fabric, including old cotton sheets or sari silk. You can even dye or paint these strips in your chosen color palette for a really custom look. See pages 52–53 for how to create your own fabric yarn from sheets.

01 Prepare your materials for weaving. If you plan to create your own T-shirt or fabric yarn, follow steps 1 and 2 on page 52. You will need to create enough yarn for both the warp and the weft, and it's always best to make more than you think you will need (extra fabric always comes in handy).

02 Stand the birch branches up in two sand-filled buckets, 4' to 6' (1.2 to 1.8 m) apart.

03 Warp the upright branches horizontally, using them as a loom. Starting at least 2' (60.9 cm) from the ground, use a surgical knot (see page 35) to tie one end of your fabric yarn around the left-hand branch; this will be

the lowest point of the backdrop. Bring the warp yarn across and around the right-hand branch, then back across, over, and around the left branch, so the yarn forms a figure eight between the two branches. Work your way up the branches, leaving 4" (10.2 cm) of space between each warp. Check your tension every couple of rows—you want it to be bouncy but not so tight that it pulls the branches together.

04 When you have warped at least 3' (91.4 cm), or as much of the branches as you want, tie the fabric yarn off around the right-hand branch with a surgical knot.

05 Using tabby stitch, weave your weft yarn vertically into the horizontal warp, starting at the bottom left. Guide your yarn over the first warp thread, under the second one, back over the third, and so on, until you reach the topmost warp thread. (A)

06 Begin your second row, working from top to bottom and making sure that this row alternates with your first row, to create a netted section between the rows of warp. Make sure to bubble each row of tabby stitch (see page

33). (B) Check your work after every few rows, beating down the stitches with your fingers to create a tighter weave—this will ensure your backdrop holds its shape well. Whenever your weft yarn grows short, add in a new piece, making sure to cross the two short tails over each other before you continue. Once you have woven the entire backdrop, pull the end of the fabric yarn through to the back of the piece, leaving a 6" (15.2 cm) tail. Weave in all the ends.

WEAVING AL FRESCO

If you plan to weave between two trees be sure to get there early, as every site is different and this project can take a bit of time to make and set up, depending on the size of your backdrop. A 4' (122 cm) square backdrop takes about an hour to weave. Another idea is to make this a communal weaving experience: set up the warp on your own and then provide a big basket of fabric strips, so your guests can help weave it together as they arrive. The beauty of this piece is that you can make it over and over again, changing the color palette to suit the event or the environment.

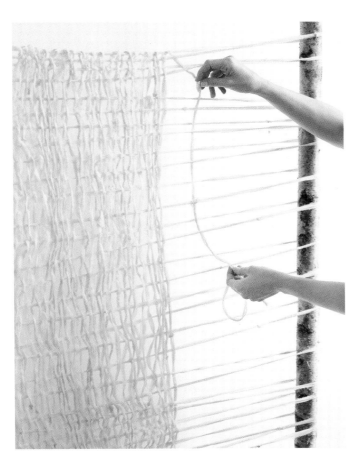

A Weave vertically into the horizontal warp using tabby stitch.

B Make sure to bubble each row of weaving, just as you would a smaller piece.

RESERVES

RESOURCES

THE MATERIALS AND TOOLS used in the projects in this book are generally available at art supply, craft, and hardware stores nationwide. If you cannot find what you are looking for locally, try these online sources:

WEAVING ESSENTIALS

I have curated a selection of tools and materials that the beginner weaver needs (and the more advanced weaver wishes for) in my Etsy shop. Look there for looms, basic tools, fibers (including cotton rug warp and specially curated weaving packs that include vintage and hand spun yarn), and sign-ups for my in-person weaving classes.

etsy.com/shop/MaryanneMoodie

FIBER SOURCES

I love to use handspun, vintage, and recycled fibers for my weavings. Here is a selection of my favorite shops:

Purl SOHO
purlsoho.com

....

Argyle Yarn Shop
argyleyarnshop.com

....

Divinity Fibers
Merino wool roving yarn, mohair
etsy.com/shop/DivinityFibers

....

Flea's Fibers
Recycled sari silk
etsy.com/shop/FleasFibers

....

Handspun Yarn Shop
Handspun wool yarn
etsy.com/shop/HANDSPUNYARNSHOP

....

Hippie Chix Fiber Art
Wool locks and non-traditional fibers
etsy.com/shop/hippiechixfiber

ADDITIONAL SOURCES

Woven Wall Hanging Sampler
Page 46
Brass rods
dickblick.com

....

Moroccan Boucherouite Rug
Page 55
Base rug
Amazon.com
T-shirt yarn
woolandthegang.com

....

Woven Necklace
Page 70
Copper rods
etsy.com/shop/OzBrassShop

....

Wrapped Lampshade
Page 86
Lampshade Frame
etsy.com
Pendant Light Kit
etsy.com or any hardware store

....

Bicycle Basket
Page 115
bikewagon.com

ACKNOWLEDGMENTS

THANK YOU TO EVERYONE who has taken the time to listen and talk, laugh and cry, encourage and give critical feedback, and learn and teach along the way.

To my family, Aaron, Murray, and little Rudi, for tolerating the fluff and the tangles.

To MM studio, Kaelyn, Blair, and Emma, for help with all of the unglamorous behind-the-scenes tasks.

To my big, beautiful extended family in Melbourne, who taught me that I was on the right track when they laughed (kindly) at every weird little weaving I created.

To Cristina and everyone at Abrams, for helping to bring this beautiful furry baby into this crazy world.

To Alexandra, Stephanie, and Kelly, for capturing my dream so perfectly in photographs.

To Sebit, for translating my work into this clean, beautiful design.

To Sophie, Virginia, and Donica, for their help in navigating the world of publishing.

To Megan Morton, who showed me the possibility of elegance and style in education.

And finally, thank you to my weaving students, for teaching me, inspiring me, and making it all worth it.

ABOUT
THE AUTHOR

MARYANNE MOODIE is a professional textile artist and teacher. She produces modern woven wall hangings for individual and corporate clients as well as teaches monthly weaving workshops around the United States and in her native Australia. Her work has been featured in *New York* magazine, *Anthology*, and *O, the Oprah* magazine, and online on *Design*Sponge* and *The Design Files*. A finalist in the Martha Stewart American Made Awards in both 2014 and 2015, she sells her work on Etsy and through online shops and boutiques around the country. In 2013, she relocated her studio from Melbourne, Australia, to Brooklyn, New York, where she continues to grow her work.

EDITOR
CRISTINA GARCES

DESIGNER
SEBIT MIN

PRODUCTION MANAGER
KATIE GAFFNEY

Library of Congress Control Number: 2015955673

ISBN: 978-1-4197-2237-0

Abrams books are available at special discounts when purchased in quantity for premiums and promotions as well as fundraising or educational use. Special editions can also be created to specification. For details, contact specialsales@abramsbooks.com or the address below.

Printed and bound in the United States
10 9 8 7 6 5 4 3 2 1

ABRAMS
The Art of Books

115 West 18th Street
New York, NY 10011
www.abramsbooks.com